The 10 Commandments of Crowdfunding

Cecelia Otto

THE 10 COMMANDMENTS OF CROWDFUNDING

Editor, Interior Design and Layout, and Cover Design:
MJ Schwader, www.InspiredLifePublications.com

Copyright © 2017 by Cecelia Otto

All rights reserved.
No part of this book may be reproduced without written permission from the publisher or copyright holder, except for a reviewer who may quote brief passages in a review; nor may any part of this book be reproduced, stored in a retrieval system, or transmitted in any form or by any means electronic, mechanical, photocopying, recording, or other, without written permission from the publisher or copyright holder.

ISBN-13: 978-1537725543
ISBN-10: 1537725548

Library of Congress Control Number: 2016917679

Dedication

For those who wish to make the impossible a certainty, this is for you. May the words of this book help you make your mark on the world, and in the process find a lasting community.

The 10 Commandments of Crowdfunding

Acknowledgments

Without the help of many fantastic people, you would not be holding this book in your hands. I'd like to thank and acknowledge them here.

To my writing coach and editor, MJ Schwader: Who knew that one conversation would lead to this? This book would not be what it is without your insights, laughs, guidance, and support these past months. I am a better writer and person because of you, and I look forward to future collaborations together.

To my wonderful husband, Dan Wiencek: After the first book, I had no idea I would have another one in me waiting to come out. Thank you for your unwavering love and belief in me, and know that I adore you, now and forever.

To all of my Kickstarter and Indiegogo backers: You have helped me produce a cross-country tour, record an album, and in turn, write this book, and I never would have achieved these goals and dreams without you. Always remember what your contribution has given me: the ability to help others all around the world in ways I don't think any of us ever imagined. Thank you!

THE 10 COMMANDMENTS OF CROWDFUNDING

TABLE OF CONTENTS

DEDICATION	**III**
ACKNOWLEDGMENTS	**V**
PREFACE	**XI**
PROLOGUE COMMANDMENT: THOU SHALT KNOW THE BASICS BEHIND CROWDFUNDING	**XIII**
WHO IS CROWDFUNDING GOOD FOR?	XIV
A FEW STATISTICS TO SET THE STAGE	XV
THE ORIGINAL TESTAMENT	**1**
COMMANDMENT I THOU SHALT DO EXTENSIVE RESEARCH ON THY CAMPAIGN PRIOR TO LAUNCH	**3**
TIMING IS KEY	5
HOW LONG SHOULD I DO RESEARCH ON MY CAMPAIGN?	7
COMMANDMENT II THOU SHALT FIND AND CREATE AN ENTHUSIASTIC COMMUNITY PRIOR TO LAUNCH	**9**
ASSESS YOUR AUDIENCE	9
FIND THE COMMON LINK	10
HOW DO I BUILD UP THIS IDEAL CROWD PRIOR TO LAUNCH?	11
COMMANDMENT III THOU SHALT PICK A PLATFORM THAT IS POPULAR AND WELL KNOWN	**13**
KICKSTARTER: THE "KLEENEX" OF CROWDFUNDING	14
HOW DOES KICKSTARTER MAKE THEIR MONEY?	16
INDIEGOGO: THE KINDER, GENTLER VERSION OF KICKSTARTER	16

The 10 Commandments of Crowdfunding

GoFundMe: This time, it's personal	17
Kickstarter Comparison Chart	18
Indiegogo Comparison Chart	19
GoFundMe Comparison Chart	19
Commandment IV Thou Shalt Set Realistic Goals	21
Commandment V Thou Shalt Be Consistent	25
Commandment VI Thou Shalt Have a Compelling Video on Thy Campaign Page	29
Commandment VII Thou Shalt Keep Thy Backers Engaged	31
The "Why"	31
Your audience reach	32
My crowd is built – how do I keep them engaged during the campaign?	32
During the campaign	33
Commandment VIII Thou Shalt Not Go It Alone	35
Pep talk for the campaign weary	36
Commandment IX Thou Shalt Use Social Media Before, During, and After the Campaign	39
Facebook for crowdfunding	40
LinkedIn for crowdfunding	41
Twitter for crowdfunding	42
YouTube for crowdfunding	43
Commandment X Thou Shalt Stay in Touch With Backers After the Campaign	45
You're successful	45
You're not successful	46
A few points to keep in mind before you re-launch	47
One final word: Keep backers engaged	48

THE 10 COMMANDMENTS OF CROWDFUNDING

BONUS SECRET COMMANDMENT THOU SHALT HAVE CLEAR
AND CONCISE MESSAGING 49

THE NEW TESTAMENT
CROWDFUNDING THE SECOND TIME 55

**THE GOSPEL OF CROWDFUNDING ACCORDING TO CECE,
CHAPTER 1:** DOING MY SECOND CAMPAIGN 57

**THE GOSPEL OF CROWDFUNDING ACCORDING TO CECE,
CHAPTER 2:** TWO-WEEK 10 COMMANDMENT CHECK-IN ... 61

**THE GOSPEL OF CROWDFUNDING ACCORDING TO CECE,
CHAPTER 3:** THE DAY BEFORE AND THE FIRST FEW DAYS OF MY
SECOND CAMPAIGN 67

**THE GOSPEL OF CROWDFUNDING ACCORDING TO CECE,
CHAPTER 4:** THE END OF THE FIRST WEEK OF MY SECOND
CAMPAIGN 75

**THE GOSPEL OF CROWDFUNDING ACCORDING TO CECE,
CHAPTER 5:** THE SECOND WEEK 79

**THE GOSPEL OF CROWDFUNDING ACCORDING TO CECE,
CHAPTER 6:** THE SEQUEL TO THE SECOND WEEK 83

**THE GOSPEL OF CROWDFUNDING ACCORDING TO CECE,
CHAPTER 7:** THE HALFWAY POINT AND OBSERVATIONS FROM
THE THIRD WEEK 87

**THE GOSPEL OF CROWDFUNDING ACCORDING TO CECE,
CHAPTER 8:** THE FINAL 10 DAYS OF THE CAMPAIGN 89

APPENDIX 99
BENCHMARKS FROM THE WHARTON CROWDFUNDING STUDY ... 99
CROWDFUNDING CAMPAIGN CHECKLIST 105
ABOUT CECE OTTO 107
DEAR READER... 108

THE 10 COMMANDMENTS OF CROWDFUNDING

Preface

Had you met me in my late 20s and told me that I would be a historian, vintage musician, and crowdfunding consultant, I would have told you that you were crazy and moved to another seat on the bus. Period.

After 2008, I was at a crossroads in my music career. I had all of this classical training, but very little to show for it. I knew that I had something to share with this world, but I didn't know what it looked like.

I did a lot of soul searching, and then settled on creating a six-month "singing travelogue" along America's first transcontinental road, the Lincoln Highway. (You can read more about it in *An American Songline: A Musical Journey Along the Lincoln Highway*). Financing this endeavor was no easy feat, so I applied for grants and corporate sponsorships. All of those applications were rejected, for I had no proof of concept. No one had done what I was proposing to do, so why would they fund me?

A few people in passing had mentioned to me that I should think about doing a Kickstarter campaign to raise the funds. With no other options, I took the plunge and launched my Kickstarter campaign in February 2013. For the next 30 days, all I thought about was trying to raise $15,000 to make my dream a reality. I had people from all over the world who were very supportive, and others who wrote me telling me, "I'm not paying for your six-month vacation!" It was exhausting reaching out to thousands of people.

At the 11th hour, I was successful. All in all, I raised $15,291 in 30 days, and I was relieved. I could now pay the musicians performing with me a decent wage, and I could afford the rental fees and liability insurance for the concerts. The best part? I could make those concerts free to the public, and now thousands of Americans could hear their history through music.

After that successful campaign, people began to ask me how I did it, and I shared my tips with them. As time went on, more and more people asked me for thoughts and help on their campaigns. It was clear I had to share these ideas with the world. I began to give presentations about the ins and outs of doing a crowdfunding campaign when I toured with *American Songline*, and I saw that there just wasn't enough time in these presentations to cover everything.

Due to the incredible interest in this topic as crowdfunding has become mainstream, I am pleased to now present you with *The 10 Commandments of Crowdfunding: The Book*!

The 10 Commandments of Crowdfunding

Prologue Commandment: Thou Shalt Know the Basics Behind Crowdfunding

I'm guessing that you probably have a vague idea of what crowdfunding is since you're reading this book, but to make sure we're all starting at the same level, I will clarify what this idea is.

The 2014 Webster's Dictionary defines crowdfunding as:

> "THE PRACTICE OF SOLICITING FINANCIAL CONTRIBUTIONS FROM A LARGE NUMBER OF PEOPLE, ESPECIALLY FROM THE ONLINE COMMUNITY."

The Oxford Dictionary has a slightly different definition:

> "THE PRACTICE OF FUNDING A PROJECT OR VENTURE BY RAISING MANY SMALL AMOUNTS OF MONEY FROM A LARGE NUMBER OF PEOPLE, TYPICALLY VIA THE INTERNET. MUSICIANS, FILMMAKERS, AND ARTISTS HAVE SUCCESSFULLY RAISED FUNDS AND FOSTERED AWARENESS THROUGH CROWDFUNDING."

I like to call it:

> "A DO-IT-YOURSELF, ONLINE PBS PLEDGE DRIVE."

THE 10 COMMANDMENTS OF CROWDFUNDING

You pitch whatever it is you are trying to raise funds for via an online page, and then, in most cases, offer some type of reward for contributions as a thank you (gifts, equity, etc.). There are several types of crowdfunding out there, and we will go into more details about that later.

WHO IS CROWDFUNDING GOOD FOR?

This is kind of a tricky question. I can tell you that crowdfunding isn't just for creative types anymore — it is for non-profits, businesses, and entrepreneurs, too. Almost everyone can benefit from crowdfunding at some point in his or her life; the question is, when does it work best?

We'll cover more ground on this in future chapters, but in essence the people who have a successful campaign are people who have a good online social presence or cause, and they want to raise money. I've had consulting sessions with people who had no online business yet, but wanted to raise money to get the capital to start the business. This is a definite no-no. I had to gently tell them to build a website, get online followers, and get known in the virtual world first before launching a campaign. The average stranger must know and understand who you are and what you stand for before you can get money from them.

I would also like to note that crowdfunding is for people who are hard workers and risk-takers. You have to be willing to put yourself out there, and do it without shame. If something with those words doesn't mesh well with you, I would strongly recommend you re-think the idea of doing this type of fundraising.

THE 10 COMMANDMENTS OF CROWDFUNDING

A FEW STATISTICS TO SET THE STAGE

In June 2015, *Parade* magazine noted the following:

> ### THE NUMBER OF WEBSITES WITH CROWDFUNDING PLATFORMS: 1,000

When I share this statistic in my talks, people are generally shocked and sometimes get even more overwhelmed than they were before I started talking. And I'm sure that number is growing every day, although we only hear about a handful of platforms. Pretty crazy, isn't it?

How do you really zero in on which platform is right for you? We'll cover that in **COMMANDMENT III: THOU SHALT PICK A PLATFORM THAT IS POPULAR AND WELL KNOWN**.

> ### THE AMOUNTS OF MONEY INTERNET USERS SPEND TO BACK CAMPAIGNS: $10 BILLION

Again, that number is much higher than most people think. While that means there's a lot of money out there to help you fund your campaign, the truth is that there are also more people out there with campaigns vying to raise money at the same time as you are.

> ### ESTIMATED NUMBER OF JOBS CREATED BY CROWDFUNDING IN 2014: 270,000

If there are people out there who think that crowdfunding won't last and isn't worthwhile, quote this statistic. There are always people out there looking for work, whether we like it or not, and your next big idea could be the answer to helping someone take care of their family.

THE 10 COMMANDMENTS OF CROWDFUNDING

THE REVENUE THAT CROWDFUNDING ADDS TO THE GLOBAL ECONOMY: $65 BILLION

This is indeed another huge number. This dollar amount is nothing to sneeze at! Imagine what even 1/10 of this amount can do for people all over the world.

In October 2015, the crowdfunding website Indiegogo published seven results they gleaned from the data gathered from 100,000 campaigns. Here's what they found:

1. 30-DAY CAMPAIGNS WORK BEST

Some campaign platforms give you the option to vary the length of campaigns (15-60 days is the normal range). Indiegogo found that the campaigns that ran anywhere from 30-39 days were the most successful. This length of time creates a sense of urgency for both you and your backers to donate and get the word out versus a longer campaign.

From personal experience running my own two campaigns and monitoring other people's campaigns, this is true. I would strongly recommend you think in terms of 30 days, if possible.

2. KEEP YOUR CAMPAIGN PAGE UPDATED

People who stay engaged with their campaigns by posting a minimum of four updates (one a week for a 30-day campaign) were more likely to have backers. We'll be discussing how to keep these backers interested and engaged in **COMMANDMENT VII: THOU SHALT KEEP THY BACKERS ENGAGED**.

3. START AND FINISH STRONG

For those 100,000 campaigns, 42% of funds were raised in the first and last three days of the campaign. That means if you have a 30-day campaign, you'll have to really think of how to keep momentum going during the other 24 days. Which leads us to #4…

4. ADD NEW PERKS AFTER THE LAUNCH

This is a fantastic way to keep momentum going during the middle of the campaign. You can see what dollar amount people are pledging at the most, and then add a new reward tier with an extra perk that's only $5-10 higher. You'd be surprised how many people will increase their dollar amount.

5. WORK WITH A TEAM

Several crowdfunding platforms will allow you to add people to your campaign page, and they can then create and post updates. By adding team members to your campaign, Indiegogo notes that your campaign will raise three times more funds than one individual will.

Logically, this makes sense right? The more people getting the word out, the more funds are likely to appear. I can tell you from personal experience, I wish I had created a team when I ran my campaign in 2013. While I was successful and raised enough money in my 30 days, I know I wouldn't have struggled as much as I did during the middle period.

We'll be talking more about this in **COMMANDMENT VIII: THOU SHALT NOT GO IT ALONE**.

6. Include a Pitch Video

If you have a video on your campaign page explaining who you are and what you do, and people can see what you're all about, you're likely to get four times more funding than those who don't have video. Spend the time to create a good video, and you will see a difference in how quickly people respond to you.

We'll be covering this topic with **COMMANDMENT VI: THOU SHALT HAVE A COMPELLING VIDEO ON THY PAGE**.

7. Maximize Your Global Reach

When considering campaign strategy, think about different time zones and target specific countries that would be interested in your campaign. Indiegogo noted that the top five countries that gave the most money to campaigns were in this order: United States, Canada, United Kingdom, Australia, and Germany.

This was something I started to think about when I started getting backers in other countries. I personally thought no one outside of the US would be interested in such a specific piece of history. I was so wrong. A man from Brazil, a Lincoln Highway aficionado who had driven the highway in 2012, saw my tweets about my campaign, and he backed me early with a $20 pledge. He said, "I know it's not much, but I sincerely hope you make it!" It blew me away, and boosted my confidence to keep moving forward.

After that, I started scheduling different social media posts to note these different time zones, and it really made a difference. Because of how crucial social media is to a successful campaign, I'll be talking about it in **COMMANDMENT IX: THOU SHALT USE SOCIAL MEDIA BEFORE, DURING, AND AFTER THE CAMPAIGN**.

Now that you've had a few numbers thrown at you, let's start strategizing on how you will collect those dollars and turn them into your dreams!

THE ORIGINAL TESTAMENT

The 10 Commandments of Crowdfunding

Commandment I
Thou Shalt Do Extensive Research on thy Campaign Prior to Launch

So you've got an idea or creative project, and you want to share it with everyone. Maybe you are a business owner, and you want to get the word out about a new product or service. Crowdfunding is an amazing way to raise awareness and funds for you and your brand.

Unfortunately, what often happens is that someone is so ambitious and idealistic with his or her ideas, they don't step back and really think through the strategy. They are desperate, and hastily throw up a campaign page, share it with their friends, and cross their fingers hoping things will turn out okay.

I'm sorry to tell you that when it comes to crowdfunding, that doesn't work, folks. Those days are long gone where you could expect someone to find you randomly. There is so much "white noise" on the Internet; you have to make sure you can bring your all to a crowdfunding campaign.

So after you're sure about your idea, I recommend everybody and anybody who's going to do a crowdfunding campaign to go on Kickstarter, Indiegogo, or whatever platform's website you'd like to run a campaign on, and see if your campaign idea has already happened. *Then* do a general Internet research to see what's out there and if something similar has already been funded.

While doing your research, take notes on each campaign and ask yourself the following questions:

- ☐ **Is there a campaign out there like what I want to do?** If so, was it successful? If it was successful, make a note of the platform and date/time of year they ran the campaign, for this can give you great insights as to what lies ahead.

- ☐ **How much funding did they get?** Pretty straightforward, but did they go over their goal? If so, how much over?

- ☐ **How many backers did they get?** Combine that with the social media following they have, and you can then estimate what kind of crowd you need to get before you launch.

- ☐ **What kinds of rewards did they give away, and which rewards/reward tiers were the most successful?** Really take your time looking at this one. Your crowd may be of a similar mindset, and it will help you figure out a final total for your overall crowdfunding budget.

- ☐ **How many updates did they do during the campaign?** Some campaigns don't need to update as much as others; it all depends on the crowd and their expectations. Regardless, you should know what kinds of updates work best for your potential backers as well.

- ☐ **What does their video look like?** We'll take time to focus a whole chapter on this, but it's important to get a sense of what they talked about in their video, as well as their overall concept. You can then take what they did, tailor it to your needs, and then make your video better than theirs.

If a similar campaign didn't get funded, look at it with the above questions in mind and figure out why. If you can't figure out why they failed, then step back and evaluate if your project should be funded using crowdfunding. I know that may sound harsh, but not everyone's ideas are cut out for this type of medium.

If you're like me and you found nothing under "singing travelogue," check similar types of campaigns. I looked at various road trip projects. Many of these campaigns didn't get funded because people thought, "Why would I pay for your extended vacation?" During my pre-launch stage, I had to really think about what language and wording I would use to explain what I was trying to do. I had to share with people that I was not going on vacation, that I would be working virtually the whole time, and that they would not be paying for my free ride. Be prepared to say, "Here's what I'm going to step up with," and create that level of trust within your community. Remember, you will need to educate them as much as you can prior to launch.

Timing is key

Timing is key when launching a campaign. If you launch on a Monday or a Tuesday, you will do better because you can build more momentum through the first week. No matter what you do, do not launch a campaign during the holiday season. There was a colleague of mine who ran a campaign during December, and he wondered why his campaign didn't get funded. Unless you have a major television spot during November or December, launch a campaign away from major holidays, so people have more of their disposable income to give to you.

You are now probably wondering when is the best time to launch a campaign. Here are my thoughts, broken down month-by-month (with typical North American holidays in mind):

The 10 Commandments of Crowdfunding

January	I'd not recommend this month. People are recovering from the holidays financially, and probably won't have the income to spare.
February	**This is a great month to launch a campaign.** People have recovered from the holidays and there are no major holidays going on, so people are more likely to give.
March	Again, this is a pretty good month, but be aware of spring break, Easter, Passover, and the like. If your demographic will be unavailable during these times, don't launch.
April	This month is pretty controversial. Some people say yes because people will have refund money from their income tax forms; others (like me) are wary of this time because of people owing money to the IRS. Again, think about your target market, and plan accordingly.
May	I think this month could work as a last resort, but you'll be competing with Mother's Day, high school/college graduations, weddings, and more.
June - August	I wouldn't bother. People are on vacation and may or may not be near their computers.
September	Probably best to not launch this month. It's back to school, and people may not have the disposable income to give you.

October	**This month is the second-best month to do a campaign.** No major holidays, and it's before the holiday season so people have plenty of cash.
November and December	Not recommended for the reasons noted above.

How long should I do research on my campaign?

I wish I had an easy answer to this question, but research will also depend on what you are doing and how big of a following you currently have. If you've got a decent following in place already, I'd plan on still giving yourself a good month to research the ins and outs of everything. If you don't have a following on social media, then plan for extra time. I'd start by building more of a following and then incorporating your research into your social media posts. Remember to get honest feedback from loyal people close to you about your business and your life; this step is important, and it will help your campaign thrive.

Now that you've got a rough idea of what's ahead, work backward from the last day of your campaign to get all of your strategies in place. You may have to work back six to twelve months depending on your situation, but the more structure you put in place, the better.

The 10 Commandments of Crowdfunding

Commandment II
Thou Shalt Find and Create an Enthusiastic Community Prior to Launch

It's easy for us to think that we're all alone in the virtual world, and that community doesn't matter. This is false. Creating a virtual community is extremely important to your campaign, for they will be the ones who are more likely to donate than friends and family.

I'm sure that's hard to read, but it's true. While friends and family are crucial to your campaign's success, you'll need to go bigger and think about how you can bring a total stranger into your fold without them ever meeting you. To do that, you're going to need to create a culture that will get people to sign up, donate, and promote you. How do you that? First, you must…

Assess your audience

Before you launch, you need to assess your audience reach, and figure out how many people you can tap into, not only as backers, but also to help you get the word out. You have to remember that not every person in your immediate circle will be able to give, so you need to cast your net wide to specific targeted groups who will most likely contribute money to your campaign.

THE 10 COMMANDMENTS OF CROWDFUNDING

Two important numbers to keep in mind:

- ☐ On the whole, your average successful campaign typically has around 150-200 backers (my first campaign had 161).

- ☐ This next figure can vary, but your next important number is your total social reach. This number is your sphere of friends, family, colleagues, customers, and more. Some experts recommend that this number be a minimum of 4,000 people who are excellent, targeted leads; they note that if you don't have this number your campaign will not be successful. I don't think this is necessarily so. I think if you have created a good culture of trust and loyalty with a smaller following, you can still be successful. I had around 2,000 people and was able to pull off a successful campaign, but note that I had been interacting with various Lincoln Highway groups for years prior to launch. Again, look at how much money you are trying to raise with the crowd you have; if you feel there's not enough people, you'll need to build your crowd up first.

FIND THE COMMON LINK

Lots of business coaches suggest this idea for new businesses starting out, and I think it works well for something like this too. Close your eyes, and imagine what your ideal crowdfunding backer looks like. How old are they? Where do they come from? What are their hobbies? What motivates and impels them to give their hard-earned dollars to people? What do your backers all have in common?

In my campaign, I imagined my backer between 35-55 years old, and they are based in the United States. They really enjoy music, history, and road trips, and they appreciate the kitsch of vintage Americana. They love spending money on travel, and they care about the preservation of America's culture and history.

Really sit and think about the backer's needs and desires first, and then create a campaign around those ideals. While you can and will attract people from all walks of life, your posts and crowdfunding page should be tailored to fit this ideal backer.

How do I build up this ideal crowd prior to launch?

As soon as you know you're going to do a crowdfunding campaign, start your research. Pick your date of launch (see previous chapter for times of year), and work backward from there to start making your plan.

You'll need to find like-minded people online who will want to back your cause and/or help promote you. Writing a book about a particular topic or thinking of launching a project? Find bloggers, Facebook groups, and forums and join them if you haven't already. Start contributing to these forums on a regular basis so that you are known and trustworthy.

You can of course bring up the idea of your book/project to see if there's a group of people who will support it, but don't come in with the hard sell right away. Find affiliate bloggers who would be willing to write something about you or let you be a guest on their blog. Follow those people on social media who could be influential; while they may not be able to contribute to your campaign, they might just help you get the word out. I had one Twitter follower who really loved the idea of the project, and was constantly tweeting and re-tweeting in support of making my campaign succeed.

About 3-6 months before you launch, you and your possible campaign teammates write everyone via all social media platforms and email in private messages informing them of the project and asking for their support when the campaign launches. Keep this letter short. Even if you have the same people on multiple platforms, reach out to them on all of them. It allows them to ask you questions if they have any, and it gives them time to refer you to affiliates and bloggers.

You will write many messages during this time, but it will be worth it. For those who show interest, do a follow up email both

30 days and 15 days prior to launch, as well as the day of the launch to let them know when the campaign will be live, and again asking for help and support. I know it seems repetitive, but a lot can happen after that first inquiry, and folks appreciate the reminder in this busy world.

If you don't have the time to manually send all of these messages and build momentum prior to launch, consider teaming with a virtual assistant or social media consultant to help you before and during the campaign. You'll of course need to budget for this, and don't use crowdfunding dollars to do so since you will need to pay these people up front.

Remember, you have to create a community that knows you, trusts you, and is willing to support you. You have to think of this as your own virtual village of people, and you all share a special culture that only you all understand. If you don't create this environment, you can still run a campaign; it just may have a harder time succeeding. Being the "early adopter" to crowdfunding, I didn't do this to the extent that I'd liked the first time, but I also had to spend a lot of time educating my public on how crowdfunding works. You are blessed to now have more awareness and acceptance of this type of fundraising, so use the extra time to create a solid following.

Commandment III
Thou Shalt Pick a Platform that is Popular and Well Known

You have your idea; you have your following that will back you; what's next? It's time to pick a platform that will help you achieve your goals. When you were doing your campaign research, you probably did some crowdfunding platform research at the same time.

Pop Quiz: How many crowdfunding platforms are out there?

- ☐ 200
- ☐ 500
- ☐ 1,000
- ☐ 2,500

Have your guess? The answer: 1,000 (and growing every day!).

I'm sure that has to feel even more overwhelming than it already does, but this is how it stands as of 2016. With that said, crowdfunding websites fall into four types:

1. **Donation-based:** Charitable contributions for a cause, and you can fund products or services.

2. **Lending-based:** These sites are for investors who want to lend money and have it paid back. The most well-known website in this arena is kiva.org.

3. **Equity-based:** Investors will back your project, and then they receive a percentage of ownership (fundable.com). Both equity- and lending-based crowdfunding platforms

became truly viable platforms in the SEC's eyes on May 16th, 2016, and I would strongly advise not using this type of platform since it is in its infancy at the time of this writing.

4. **Reward or Pledge-based:** This type of platform is the most popular of the four options, and gets the most social media traffic. These websites are for projects or companies who have an item or service, and you're willing to give something in exchange for contributions.

Because of the online visibility and current popularity of reward-based campaigns, this book will generally focus on this group. If you are thinking about doing a campaign with one of the other groups, please feel free to contact me directly to see what your options are. The rules are shifting so much in some of these other groups that I'd rather not write about them so that I don't give you misinformation.

Within the reward-based groups, we are going to narrow the focus to three websites: Kickstarter, Indiegogo, and GoFundMe. These three websites have more web traffic than all of the others out there combined, and if you're looking to get more exposure to the world, your best bet is to use one of these. For the record, I do not endorse one site over another – each platform is a little different and one will suit your needs better than another one.

KICKSTARTER:
THE "KLEENEX" OF CROWDFUNDING

One of my clients used the above metaphor for Kickstarter, and I loved it. When most Americans reach for a facial tissue, they call it a Kleenex®. They call almost all facial tissues by this brand name, and everyone knows what it means. Kickstarter has this same status in the crowdfunding world. When people hear the word "Kickstarter," they know what it means. This can be a good thing, but sometimes it can cause problems for the average person who knows nothing about crowdfunding. People tend to think that

ALL crowdfunding platforms operate in the same way that Kickstarter does, and that's simply not true.

Here's how the Kickstarter platform operates: Have a creative project or need something for your business that has a clear goal or endgame in mind? This is a requirement for Kickstarter. They do not allow you to fundraise for charity or for financial incentives or equity in a company.

A perfect example of a project for Kickstarter was my American Songline project. I wanted to do a singing travelogue tour, and I needed funds to help make the concerts free to the public. Note that I was not trying to get money for never-ending performances; it was for just this one period of time. I find that all creative types (authors, musicians, inventors) really align well with this platform, and even some businesses can use it too.

But there's a catch:

IT IS ALL OR NOTHING!

What does that mean? This means that when you set up your campaign goal amount (let's use $10,000 for this example), you must meet your goal within the prescribed amount of time (1-60 days), or you get nothing. That's right. You could have $9,999.99, and if you're off by that penny when your campaign ends, you won't get any of that money. This high pressure system works – campaign creators have a lot to lose, so they give it their all and keep their backers engaged. It's also important to note that the higher the risk, the higher the credibility. When people find out I was successful on Kickstarter versus any other platform, they take me seriously. And that's a credibility no one can take away from you.

The 10 Commandments of Crowdfunding

How does Kickstarter make their money?

If you are successful, they will take 5% of your earnings as their cut. Pledges are taken out using a third-party payment company called Stripe, and they usually charge between 3-5% for their payment processing fees. So this means you need to budget around 8-10% of your funds earned to go back to these outlets – you have been warned. If your campaign is not successful, neither Kickstarter nor Stripe takes any money from you or your backers.

There are a lot more rules when it comes to getting your project and campaign approved by Kickstarter, so please read through everything carefully before you send them anything, as policies can and will change. If your project is accepted, know that you will be tapping into the biggest online community who supports crowdfunding projects, which is at 10 million people currently and growing every day.

Author's note: As of June 2016, Kickstarter now allows more than one campaign creator email address tied to the campaign. In the past, only one email was allowed, which often led to multiple people logging in under the same email address (security nightmare to be sure), or that one person has to be the person solely responsible for the campaign. While I think this change is a very good one, I've not seen it in action since I have not run a campaign on Kickstarter since it was implemented.

Indiegogo: the kinder, gentler version of Kickstarter

I'm sure you probably laughed when you read that header, but I think it's a true statement for them. With the three main platforms we're talking about here, Indiegogo was the earliest to come on the scene in 2007 (Kickstarter was 2009). There are fewer rules when it comes to Indiegogo, and they give you more flexibility in your fundraising. You can do a campaign here and you can note it on your page. Don't have a specific project in mind?

That's okay. You can raise funds for anything personal, creative, entrepreneurial, or non-profit.

If you decide to do a campaign with them, you have the option to do either a fixed funding option (all-or-nothing like Kickstarter) or a flexible funding option, which means you get to keep everything that you earned, even if you don't meet your goal. If you are new to the idea of crowdfunding and feel a little skittish about the whole idea, Indiegogo would be a great fit for you. Campaigns can run at any length, but the most successful ones on this platform are between 30-39 days.

The fee structure works roughly the same on this platform as it does Kickstarter. They used to have different percentages when it came to flexible/fixed, but in July 2015 they moved to a flat 5% for all campaigns, plus additional third-party transaction fees that are around 3-5%. They interface with both PayPal and credit cards, so it also gives the backer more payment options than Kickstarter does.

One perk I like about Indiegogo is that you can assign team members to help you oversee your campaign. This is huge! I can tell you from experience that it's better to have help with something like this, so the more people helping you with your campaign, the more likely you are to raise whatever money you need successfully.

While Indiegogo's community is not as big as Kickstarter's, it still has a pretty substantial amount of people. I would feel more comfortable doing a campaign on this platform now versus even a few years ago. The audience has really increased on this site.

GoFundMe: This Time, It's Personal

Sorry, I couldn't help myself with that header! GoFundMe was created in 2010, and it's typically a crowdfunding platform used by people to raise money for himself or herself, a friend, or a loved one. People fundraise for medical expenses, education costs, volunteer programs, youth sports, funerals and memorials – even animals and pets. Non-profit 501c3 organizations can use this platform as well.

Like with Indiegogo, you can do either all-or-nothing or flexible funding campaigns, but people usually go with the flexible option. Fees are 5% plus a 3% transaction fee in the US and Canada (other countries, please check their website to see your transaction fees).

You can do rewards with this platform, but most people generally just do cash donations, instead of looking for a return on their investment. Out of the three platforms talked about here, this is really the only one where the audience expects no kitschy tote bags or t-shirts in return. I also really like that there are no time limits or deadlines. I personally think it's a better option for charities and people doing charitable contributions because you can leave your campaign open for as long as you need to.

If you're still unsure as to which of these platforms would be the best fit, take a look at the following comparisons:

Kickstarter Comparison Chart

Types of Campaigns	Funding Option	Fees	Payment Processor	Social Reach	Other Info
Creative projects that can be shared with others; project must have an end goal	Fixed only	Fee: If U.S. campaign is successful: 5% Payment processing fees: 3% + $0.20 per pledge. Pledges under $10 have a discounted micro pledge fee of 5% + $0.05 per pledge. Fees vary by country	Stripe Payments	The biggest of them all, with millions of followers all over the world	Has strict guidelines for projects; campaign must be approved by Kickstarter prior to launch

THE 10 COMMANDMENTS OF CROWDFUNDING

INDIEGOGO COMPARISON CHART

TYPES OF CAMPAIGNS	FUNDING OPTION	FEES	PAYMENT PROCESSOR	SOCIAL REACH	OTHER INFO
Almost any project or cause, whether personal, professional, or creative can be on this site. Non-profits can raise funds, and can also be eligible for a "badge" on their page	Fixed and flexible options are available. If initial campaign is successful, you are then eligible for "InDemand," which enables you to raise more funds whenever you see fit	Fee: U.S. campaign: 5% Payment processing fees: 3% + $0.30 per credit card transaction 2-3% for PayPal International transactions may incur added fees	Stripe Payments and PayPal	Campaigns can be run in over 200 countries in several languages, far more than Kickstarter. Social reach is not as big as Kickstarter, but they still have a pretty big following online	No review is required prior to launch

GOFUNDME COMPARISON CHART

TYPES OF CAMPAIGNS	FUNDING OPTION	FEES	PAYMENT PROCESSOR	SOCIAL REACH	OTHER INFO
You can raise money for anything on this platform; most people raise funds for personal expenses. (medical bills, funerary expenses, etc.). Charities can also raise funds	Flexible; you keep whatever you earn	Fee: U.S. & Canada: 5% Payment processing fees: 2.9% + $0.30 per transaction Certified Charities: 5%, plus 4.25% processing fees	U.S./Canada: WePay For charities: FirstGiving	You'll see GoFundMe in the news, but it's not as popular as the other two platforms	There are no time limits with this platform; it can remain active as long as you need or want it to be

The 10 Commandments of Crowdfunding

Commandment IV
Thou Shalt Set Realistic Goals

When I was first thinking about doing an American Songline Kickstarter campaign, I approached a mentor, who happened to be active in the arts scene in the Chicago area, and was a prolific grant writer. She knew all of the ins and outs of doing a project of this magnitude, and the fact that she was willing to consult pro bono for me was a very big deal. Our conversation went like this:

"So, how much do you think you will need to do this?" she asked.

"Honestly, I'm thinking about $25,000 in total from start to finish," I replied.

"That's what I was thinking," she said. "Do you think you can get that much?"

"I'm not sure. That's a year's salary to some people."

Remember, my campaign ran in early 2013, which believe it or not, was still considered the "early days" of crowdfunding. I knew I'd be taking a big risk by doing this, and I wasn't sure who would back me. After our conversation, I went home and really thought about what was realistic for me, but then I also thought about what is realistic for other people. Would I have been able to use the $25,000 for the project? Sure! Was it reasonable to think I could raise it? Probably not.

I knew $10,000 would probably not get all of the performances from coast-to-coast, so I decided to go with $15,000 as a campaign goal. There were 14 states along the Lincoln Highway, and I wanted to do at least one performance in each state, hopefully more. That way, once Kickstarter and Amazon payments took their cut (Amazon payments was the third-party payment processor at the time), I'd have enough left over to cover venue rental, musicians' fees, liability insurance for every event, etc.

Even though times have changed since that campaign, I share my story with you in order for you to know and understand this commandment does still apply even today. It's not just about setting a realistic campaign goal, but you'll need to set realistic goals for your budget, your team of people helping you – in everything you do. I don't say all of this to be a "Debbie Downer"; I say this for you to be prepared for what lies ahead.

When I speak about crowdfunding to groups, I love using the reference:

> **"SHOOTING FOR THE MOON...
> WHEN YOU NEED TO GET THE ROCKET SHIP FIRST."**

As a creative and/or entrepreneur, you always dream big. You have a vision of the full picture and you want to get it out there. But depending on what you're envisioning, it may have to be imagined into smaller goals for the rest of the world. Sometimes, a lower amount for your campaign actually might be better. Also, remember that even when you meet your goal, people can still contribute to your campaign while it's still active and running.

Psychologically, people are not necessarily looking at your total on your campaign page, they're looking at how far that progress meter has gone up to see how much money you've raised. The bigger the gap that's there, the less likely they will contribute. People want to be part of something that's winning, and if it looks like it's not going to happen, then they don't want to be a part of it.

Surprisingly, people will contribute up to 30% more after you've met your goal. For average people who aren't celebrities trying to crowd-fund, you've got to be more aware of the people giving you pledges. I consulted with someone who wanted to open a non-profit preschool for disadvantaged youth. They needed to raise all of this money, including some money for playground equipment. I advised them to do one campaign for one or two pieces of equipment for their first campaign, and then build everything from there. You can do multiple campaigns after you've proven your success. Again, don't go for the whole playground; aim for the merry-go-round.

The 10 Commandments of Crowdfunding

Commandment V
Thou Shalt Be Consistent

I realize that this commandment may seem obvious too, but it's amazing how such a simple word can make all the difference.

We live in an age where pop-up ads immediately stop our trains of thought. The human brain is processing more and more information every day, and it gets overloaded all the time. Our brains are amazing machines and adapt where they can, but there's still overwhelm. The mind needs a "break" from all of this data coming at us, and how does it get that break?

Consistency.

Yes, you read that right.

The more consistent you are, the better. I'll use an example from my own travels.

When I set out along America's first transcontinental road, I had books, printed maps, online maps (when I actually had Internet access), GPS – you name it, I had it. You see, while this road was America's "Main Street" for decades, it is now a mix of national roads, county roads, even dirt tracks. It was a daunting task to think about getting across 14 states with such a hodgepodge of information.

At first, I had the hardest time. Getting across New Jersey without using the turnpike? My GPS wouldn't hear of that! Taking this "trip back in time" was way more difficult than I first realized. For you see, 100 years ago, all this country had was that *one* good road to follow; they didn't have any other roads at all.

And then I remembered something from an earlier Lincoln Highway convention I attended. A veteran of the highway told us on a tour to "look out for the telephone poles, for that would indicate the route."

While this wasn't the case all of the time in those 3,389 miles, it was a good rule of thumb. The telephone came into popularity right around the time when the road was being built, so they built the telephone lines near the best roads possible so they could easily repair and update them. Once I remembered that piece of history, if I ever got lost all I had to do was look to see where the phone poles were. I drove further west, and then Lincoln Highway signs with specific color schemes started accompanying the poles. With these consistent markers, I knew right away if I was not on the Lincoln Highway anymore, and if I got lost I could easily find my way back "home." By the end of the trip, I could feel what was the right way without looking at a single map. These small things to look for made me feel safe, and if I felt safe, I knew I could keep moving forward.

Whether you are raising money for an invention, art project, or a piece of equipment, these same principles apply. Imagine you go to a person's campaign page to check out their project and you like what you see. You then see they've got a Facebook page, as well as a website, and then you head over to those pages to find out more information. After all, you want to be an informed person before you back any project, right?

You land on their Facebook page, and something feels different. Maybe the color scheme is different, or the wording of their social media posts doesn't match the tone of the campaign page. Maybe they haven't put up a post about the campaign. Would you know if you are in the right place?

You then head over to the website, and again, everything looks different from everything you've seen before. How would this make you feel? Would you want to back someone who can't even give you basic guideposts to get you from point A to point B? I'm guessing you'd be nervous and feel uncomfortable about it.

The right side of our brain remembers all of those images, colors, and other things that our left side either can't use or takes for granted. The key is to get both halves of the brain engaged, and then things become easier.

I could list off a bunch of ways that you can make everything consistent for your campaign page, but that would take up way too much time, and frankly, you probably don't need it. I think the important themes to remember with consistency are:

1. The look – Do your color schemes on your campaign video/page match all of your other online pages? Does your profile picture match on every page too? Since they may or may not know you in real life, you need to reassure people that you are who you are, and using that same picture is necessary.
2. Wording – What kind of message do you want to share with the world? Have these words or phrases been incorporated into every way possible?
3. Video – Your campaign video must have the two elements listed above, along with your sparkly personality. ☺ If you plan on doing multiple videos throughout the campaign, keep the same length of time as much as possible.
4. Social Media – We'll be tackling this in depth in a separate chapter, but this part of your work must be the most consistent. Schedule posts prior to launch with the same link, wording, and hashtags. Post daily, and comment often.

Remember, you want people to find those "telephone poles" that help them know it's you. Parting with money is hard for some people, and the more consistency and re-assuredness you can give them, the more likely they will want to follow and back you.

The 10 Commandments of Crowdfunding

Commandment VI
Thou Shalt Have a Compelling Video on Thy Campaign Page

Video. You may love it or you may hate it, but either way, video is an important aspect to communicating these days. Words are powerful, but let's face the fact that we live in a visual society, especially in an online world. If people can see you and hear you on their computer or mobile device, they are more likely to connect with you, trust you, believe in you, and back what you want to do.

As noted in the prologue, Indiegogo did research on 100,000 crowdfunding campaigns in 2015, and found that if a campaign had a video on their page, they were four times more likely to receive funding. This once again confirms that if you want people to back you, you need to create a video that captures who you are, as well as keeping your potential backers interested.

Here are my tips on how to create a compelling video for your main campaign page:

1. Be in the video. People want to see the face of the campaign – they want to see the human side of this project/invention/cause. If you're afraid of doing this, figure out why. You are passionate about your campaign, so what's holding you back from talking to others?
2. Write a script for what you want to say in the video (how do you want to pitch people). Even those of us who are comfortable in front of people and a camera can get nervous or forget things to say, so writing out what you want to say helps get your ideas in order.

3. Read that script out loud – over and over again. Reading through it once does not cut it. Really know and embrace what you are saying. Put your all into it!
4. Once you feel comfortable reading it, have someone close to you time you. Read it in front of them like you were having a regular conversation in their living room.
5. If the speech is under three minutes, great! Anywhere from 2-3 minutes is a decent length of time for a crowdfunding campaign video. If it's over that amount of time, consider where you may want to trim down. You can always use that extra content for campaign updates during the campaign.
6. After you've trimmed down, repeat the process again.
7. When it gets to a length that you like, think about what images or music you might want to accompany your message. It doesn't have to be you the whole time. Check out other campaign videos for examples. Make sure you honor the copyrights of any music or art you use with your video.
8. Record yourself giving your pitch with the 2-3 minute script you've created. A video camera is always nice, but it is not necessary. Most smartphones have decent quality.
9. Edit your video, adding in those extra images and music you'd like to incorporate. There are tons of free video editing software out there, or if you don't want to do this part, consider hiring someone to do it.
10. Watch your final video with a few close friends and family to get any final comments or feedback, and then upload the video to your campaign page. After you launch, watch the views and the dollars roll in!

If you have other social media pages or a website, make sure you upload this video (and any other video about the campaign) directly to those pages with a link to the campaign. You will get more organic social reach (i.e. more views) on these videos, and people will be more aware of you in these mediums. If all of this still seems paralyzing after reading this, then get help! That person or persons can give you an outside perspective that could help your campaign in ways you didn't see possible.

Commandment VII
Thou Shalt Keep Thy Backers Engaged

When I speak to people, at least one person comes up to me at every talk, and they will usually say, "I'm so amazed that random people will give other random people money without question. How is that possible?"

The "Why"

The answer is simple: people want to be part of something that's bigger than themselves. I know it sounds crazy, but it's true. As our world gets smaller and faster through massive advances in technology, we as humans feel lost in it all sometimes. We have social media pages, blogs, and online journals, but the yearning to connect with others and make a difference is still important to the human experience. Crowdfunding gives a person that chance. They can pledge whatever dollar amount online from the comfort of their home and know that when that campaign or person succeeds, they can say, "I helped make this happen." It's a strong feeling that is deep within all of us that often gets overlooked.

Unsure if you know this feeling? Close your eyes, and remember the last time you sang "Happy Birthday" with a big group of people. Think about the feelings you felt when you sang it with everyone. You weren't caring about how your voice sounded, you didn't look at other people wondering if you sang it right, you just did it. For one moment, you and everyone else were all united in helping someone share in the joy of their life. You made their life better with this one small gesture, and that's the powerful feeling of crowdfunding.

Your audience reach

We covered this in great detail in Commandment Two, but here are some highlights to keep in mind for backer engagement.

Remember the two points I made on page 10 about the number of backers an average successful campaign has (150-200), and what your total outreach needs to be (4,000 excellent, targeted leads). Have you connected with those like-minded communities and bloggers online as well? While I know all of these points have been set in place long before you hit the launch button, there's always still time to find and connect with people online *while* the campaign is running.

Many social media platforms now have metrics to track interactions online; you need to be checking those several times a day during the campaign. You'll see very quickly which types of posts are working, so if you have to rewrite anything you can do that mid-stream.

My crowd is built – how do I keep them engaged during the campaign?

This should come as no surprise, but social media is crucial when it comes to making a campaign successful. You must be consistent in posting. Do not "set it and forget it." While you can use social media schedulers to help you plan and post to various pages, you need to be monitoring these pages multiple times a day, every day.

Think of your campaign being kind of like a newborn baby. You need to give it a lot of love and attention during those 30 days. My husband and I lived and breathed my campaign, and there were nights with little sleep. We deliberately didn't make any plans that month, we didn't go on a trip part way through; we stayed home and worked on it when we weren't working on our jobs. Running a campaign is a full-time job. Be honest with yourself. If you can't take on the full-time job of doing a campaign at the time you want to do it, either step back and wait to do it, or get people (paid or unpaid) to help you.

When you hit the dreaded plateau (and it will happen on everyone's campaign), don't panic. Create a new reward tier that will entice people to pledge more and get the word out. Maybe there's a new virtual reward you can create that you'll give to everyone for free once you hit a certain goal. This is a perfect time to do a video update and show all of that wonderful passion you have for what you are doing. Remember, people want to feel those powerful feelings of crowdfunding throughout the campaign, so take care of them and make yourself three-dimensional on that two-dimensional screen. The more you show up for your backers, the more your backers will show up for you.

During the campaign

Hitting the "launch" button on my campaign was one of the scariest things I've ever done in my life, and I've climbed mountains and rode horseback through Mongolia! Once you hit that button, there is no turning back. Whether you are successful with your campaign or not, your life will permanently change.

If you've done your homework, and applied everything in the earlier chapters to your pre-launch, you will be pretty much ready when this day comes. You have all the people and tools in place to keep your backers engaged. Even with everything in place, you must remember that this campaign is your full-time job. You may have to remind friends and family that you need the time to make this successful, so social plans might have to be put on hold.

If you are reading this and you've hit that dreaded plateau (days 7-23), don't lose hope. There is plenty of time to regroup and evaluate everything. Which reward tiers are getting the most backers? Consider creating a new reward tier that's $5-10 higher, add a free digital product to it, and post an update to all your backers noting that this new reward tier is now available. Many people will probably make that leap to help you.

I'd also consider adding another free product to all reward tiers if people help you meet your goal (i.e. a free MP3 or PDF or something like that). If you sweeten the pot with an additional perk that's enticing, your crowd will get the word out about these new additions, and you will hopefully get more backers.

Weekly updates with a personal touch are extremely important. Whether you are writing a post or creating a video update, the key is to make this sound as personable and positive as possible. If you stay truthful and upbeat, your enthusiasm will shine through and your backers will appreciate it. I recommend keeping updates concise, so your messaging can remain clear (see the messaging commandment if you're stuck).

Remember through all of this, your social media updates have to be consistent, so if you do make any changes you need to alert all of your followers as well. Keep using those hashtags (especially on Twitter) so people can keep finding you. Remember, the more people who find you, the better the chances are you will get funded.

Commandment VIII
Thou Shalt Not Go It Alone

I'm pretty guilty of doing a lot of things by myself, and we're encouraged to do things alone in this independent society. That's more heroic right? We like the tale of one person beating everything against the odds, and they complete their mission to the accolades of the on-looking crowds waving and throwing flowers at their feet.

Being a lone ranger is bogus. Let go of this ideal. The key word is ideal. It's not real. While you are the one who created this project or have this idea, you do not live in a vacuum. You are creating a campaign to reach out to other people, so you need to get outside perspectives on what you are doing.

If we use the same movie metaphor, some of our strongest stories about heroism all had a team behind them. Frodo Baggins had a team of people, and so does the captain of the Starship Enterprise. They could not have succeeded in their missions without the help of others, and neither should you.

As you're doing your campaign research, you'll find people who want to help and give of their time toward your cause. I think of them as ambassadors for your campaign and you. They may be family members or friends, or they might be people in a Facebook group or blogger community. Either way, once you find those people, don't let go of them. They will have a commitment and tenacity to help you that can't be bought. They will keep you on your goals. And remember, they are the people you must keep in mind when the going gets rough.

If you do decide to use Indiegogo as your platform, this is your reminder that you can assign team members to help with your campaign and campaign updates, and I recommend you take that opportunity to do so in the months prior to launch. Give them defined roles that won't overextend you or them when it's crunch time. Draw on your team's strengths. Maybe one person is better at social media, and one is better with shooting video. Leverage that – it may get them noticed too!

If you really feel like your back is against the wall and you can't tap into your close circle of people around you, consider hiring someone to help you before and/or during your campaign. Be prepared to pay these people in advance for their time; do not pay them once your campaign is finished. Consultants in crowdfunding, video, and social media would be the first people I'd consider reaching out to. Marketing people could work as well, but they need to have a certain skill set in working with this type of intense medium.

Pep talk for the campaign weary

Hi campaign creator! I wanted to let you know that I have been where you have been before, and I'm here for you in spirit. You're probably exhausted and annoyed with some of your friends and family right now, like I was, for you're now seeing people who you thought would back you aren't backing you like they promised. If that's true, I'm sorry to hear it. You have to remember that you can't take it personal, and you must keep going. There will be random strangers who may criticize you on social media, and you have to let that go, too. Remember all of the fantastic people who *are* supporting you right now, for they are the people who you must spend your time on.

If you're tired of thinking about that dollar amount and where it is right now, think about how many new backers you can get per day instead. Make it a game with you and your teammates. If you have the wherewithal, you might even think about challenging your backers to get more people to back you, and then in turn reward them for their efforts.

I had difficulty sleeping during my 30-day campaign, and I found it hard to step away from my computer. Remember to take time to breathe, and if you're stressed, to take a break. No really, take a break. Don't go on an extended vacation or anything like that, but take a few hours away and do something that has nothing to do with your campaign. Take time to unplug; go to a movie, take a walk, get a massage, and focus on something away from your laptop. Trust me, everyone will understand, and you will be rested and recharged. As I said before, the passion for your project or cause must shine through in everything that you do, and whatever break you need to get that enthusiasm back, do it. You are your greatest asset during this time, and you will do great. No matter what happens, be proud of what you've done and remember that the work you are doing in this world is awesome.

THE 10 COMMANDMENTS OF CROWDFUNDING

Commandment IX
Thou Shalt Use Social Media Before, During, and After the Campaign

Because you are working in a virtual environment raising funds, your social media has to be consistent and very interactive. Having your social media plan implemented before you launch is critical. That way, you are not as overwhelmed once the campaign begins. If you can schedule your posts with a scheduler, do it. Doing this one action will save you so much time, and potentially so much money. There are several versions of schedulers out there; some are free and some are paid services. If you have a business page on Facebook, you can also use their internal scheduler to schedule posts free of charge. I generally have good luck with their scheduler. If you use Twitter, I would advise getting some type of scheduler since you can't be posting on Twitter multiple times a day. If you don't use Twitter, I strongly recommend reviewing the Twitter section below to see why you may need to use it during your campaign.

Without further ado, here are some tips on how to use social media during your crowdfunding campaign…

The 10 Commandments of Crowdfunding

Facebook for Crowdfunding

DO...

- ☐ Make sure your business page is completely filled out and up-to-date. Your "Bio" and "About" sections should be easy to understand and read, and remember to reference back to your website in that area as well.

- ☐ Use your personal page to thank people. Don't forget to tag them in those posts too, so their friends can see your campaign info.

New to tagging? It's pretty simple. On Facebook, you'll be able to tag people on your personal page posts, but not on your business page. This is actually okay, for there's a better chance that people will actually see your post. You'll go to update your status, and when you start to type the person's name, a little pop up box will appear with a list of names below what you're typing, and you'll want to choose the person's name. Make sure their name is highlighted in blue; that way you know they're tagged properly. Type your post and publish it, and watch the comments and contributions come in. Each platform is a little different, but the premise is the same.

After you tag those people in your posts, they and their friends will see those posts. The people who contributed to your campaign will appreciate the public thank-you, and those who haven't donated yet will be more inclined to donate to your campaign if their friend on Facebook has already done so.

When someone gave me this tip of tagging people during the middle of my campaign, I didn't believe this person at first. I honestly thought it wasn't going to make a difference. After I did my first post on Facebook tagging people, I saw the contributions go up dramatically. I was surprised at how quickly it worked. To me, I think there's some psychological "peer pressure" at work here. I think on a subconscious level, people feel encouraged into rallying together to give more; they may even feel guilty, too. *If this person donated, maybe I should too?* I know it sounds blunt, but use that to your advantage in your social media posts.

- Upload your campaign videos to your Facebook page, too. You are likely to get a better organic reach on your campaign, since Facebook has so many users.

DON'T...

- Beg for money in public posts. If you must ask for money, do it in a private message, or ask if you can call them.

- Get negative or down on people. Remember, you must assume that your friends and family may not step up to the plate and help you.

- Forget to keep people updated. Facebook's algorithms change all the time, so you must post more than once during the campaign to let people know what's happening.

LINKEDIN FOR CROWDFUNDING

The "dark horse" of social media, LinkedIn is often overlooked. Don't rule this page out! In regards to tips, I would use all of the Facebook tips and apply them to your LinkedIn page. Since people may or may not read their LinkedIn feeds, I recommend taking the time to send every person you're connected to a private message both before and during the campaign. That message gets delivered to their inbox, and I've had people respond back to me via this platform over Facebook or Twitter. Some social media schedulers do let you interface with LinkedIn, so I would recommend scheduling whatever posts you can and then periodically checking in to see if anyone's responded.

THE 10 COMMANDMENTS OF CROWDFUNDING

TWITTER FOR CROWDFUNDING

DO...

- ☐ Tweet, re-tweet, and tweet some more! You cannot post too much on this platform.

- ☐ Thank people publicly on this platform, too, by tagging them with their Twitter handles. Again, they will appreciate the shout out, and you'll have more coverage of your campaign. The tweets can look something like this:

    "Thanks to @Am_Songline @MJSchwader @kickstarter @Indiegogo & @gofundme for donating to my #crowdfunding campaign! Donate here: (Link)"

    You of course would change out the @Names, but you need to make sure those are present in order for them to receive the notification that they were thanked publicly.

- ☐ Hashtag every tweet. Yes, I said it. Some generations hate this word, and others are fine with it. Regardless of your stance, hashtagging on Twitter is vital to your campaign's success. For those of you who don't know what a hashtag is, it's an important way for your tweets to be found. People on Twitter can do searches under certain words, and they will do this with a hashtag (#), the pound sign on your phone. For example, I used the hashtag #LincolnHighway and #Kickstarter often in my tweets, and I had complete strangers find my project and me, and give me money.

- ☐ Use your 140 characters wisely. Aim for 100-120 characters per tweet; that way your followers have space to write a message in before they re-tweet your tweet.

The 10 Commandments of Crowdfunding

DON'T...

- ☐ Underestimate the power of Twitter. I raised a significant portion of my funds, and was able to book performances with this medium in 30 days. If you don't use this platform or don't feel comfortable doing this platform, I would recommend you hire someone to help you set up and run your Twitter page during your campaign.

- ☐ Ignore Twitter once you sign up. Check in once a day and interact with those followers!

YouTube for Crowdfunding

If you have built up the culture via video and have a decent following on YouTube, keep doing this! You can do your weekly updates via video. And you can do more than one video per week. If you plan on implementing more video for your campaign, be sure to have a good outline of what you'll say and when.

A gentle reminder – post your videos on all platforms as original content, don't just post to YouTube and re-share it to Facebook and Twitter. Doing this will make your organic reach online go down, so when you create a video, upload it to all social networks you have business and personal pages for (i.e. Facebook, Twitter, etc.). It will seem tedious, but in the long run will really help you get noticed.

There are many social media sites out there, as you all know, but if you focus on the platforms above, you can get a decent following and get your campaign funded successfully.

On a personal note, my Kickstarter campaign would have been a disaster if I had not used social media, and this is the one area where I know I can improve on when I do it again. I will do way more work prior to launch on getting the word out via social media, and I will spend months doing so to get ready for it. I will take the time to find and follow people, and nurture those relationships with people before that launch. Find the time to do this, and you will reap the rewards.

Commandment X
Thou Shalt Stay in Touch with Backers After the Campaign

You did it! The campaign is over. Hopefully, if you did the strategies outlined earlier in this book, everything was successful. If not, skip to the next section.

You're successful

If everything went as planned, you're now officially funded, and then some. Here's what happens next:

- ☐ Various monetary transactions will start happening immediately. If you opted to do an all-or-nothing campaign, the pledges will be collected from the backers over the next few days. Note that if you had international backers, it can take even longer to collect their pledges. One of my biggest backers was from Norway, and it took weeks to get his pledge processed.

- ☐ Sticking to your budget is key. If you raised a hypothetical $25,000, about $2,000 will get taken out automatically from the crowdfunding platform (Kickstarter, Indiegogo, GoFundMe) and the payment processing company used by the platform. Sometimes, people's pledges don't ever process, and you will have to go without those donations. I am lucky to say that my campaign didn't have those issues, but I've heard of this happening to others.

THE 10 COMMANDMENTS OF CROWDFUNDING

- ☐ If you didn't send an update to your backers right as the campaign ended, do it right now. Seriously. I'll wait... It is so crucial to touch base with everyone once everything is over. Not only do you need to thank them for their support and generosity, but you also need them to confirm their mailing addresses if a reward is being sent to them.

- ☐ Once funds start appearing in your account, you should buy your supplies for your rewards, and start getting those rewards packaged and sent out right away. I recommend going to the post office during off-peak hours if possible. We made several trips to the post office for my campaign, and one receipt was over eight feet long.

- ☐ If rewards are delayed for any reason, keep your backers in the loop. People are way more understanding than you think.

- ☐ Remember, your campaign page will be ranked high in search engines when people try to find you. You will need to update your campaign page periodically to note new websites, products, etc. This page is a powerful marketing tool; use it.

- ☐ Last but not least – this is a MAJOR accomplishment. Not many people have the courage to do what you just did, so tell people your story. And then tell it again. No one can take this campaign away from you. Remember that.

YOU'RE NOT SUCCESSFUL

If you are reading this, it's because you did an all-or-nothing campaign and you didn't raise the funds you needed. If this happened, I'm truly sorry to hear this news. I am sure you feel extremely frustrated after all of the time and hard work you've put into it. But don't lose hope. The good thing is that most platforms will allow you to re-launch your campaign again if it wasn't successful; all you have to do is wait and make sure the new campaign is approved again, and then you can re-launch it at anytime.

A FEW POINTS TO KEEP IN MIND BEFORE YOU RE-LAUNCH

- ☐ Reflect on the last few weeks, and really analyze what didn't go right. Did you feel like something didn't go the way you wanted to? How many backers did you get?

- ☐ Feeling stuck and not sure what happened? You can ask friends and colleagues for their thoughts, but this is a great time to get an outside objective perspective on what could have happened. I'm happy to help you dissect everything, but the key is to find someone who is not personally attached to you and isn't invested in your campaign like you are.

- ☐ Once you've thought about everything, post an update to your backers telling them what your next steps will be. They do need to be thanked and kept in the loop, especially when the going gets tough. People will resonate with your honesty, and who knows? Maybe someone unexpected will step forward and help you.

- ☐ As noted in the previous section of this chapter, this page will appear on all search engines. It is very important that you try to keep this page current so people can find you.

- ☐ Even if you didn't get to your goal, your courage to do something like this will not go unnoticed. You don't get to brag about winning the campaign; you get to brag about running a campaign. It is not easy to do this! You have a unique set of skills that the average population doesn't have, and you can now use those skills to your business and personal advantage.

THE 10 COMMANDMENTS OF CROWDFUNDING

ONE FINAL WORD: KEEP BACKERS ENGAGED

No matter if you met your goal or didn't, you still have an obligation to keep your backers engaged long after the campaign is over. You've created this group of people who believe in you, and that needs to be cherished and nurtured. As we become more virtual in the 21st century, any online relationships need to be maintained. You never know where life will take you, and these people could become your best ally. I know that I have 161 people (183 with donations that came in after the campaign) who know me, trust me, and believe in me. That is amazing, and if I could hug and thank them every day, I would.

Good luck to you in your journey ahead, and if you ever need help, reach out to me!

Bonus Secret Commandment
Thou Shalt Have Clear and Concise Messaging

But wait, there's more!!

I couldn't help myself on that one… saying there are Ten Commandments in a book has such a nice iconic ring, doesn't it? I wanted to frame everything in that way to the world. But the Spinal Tap fan in me notes everything is better when it "goes to 11." So here's an extra commandment to think about as you're getting ready for your campaign.

As you can guess, one could write a whole book on this commandment alone. People write books on messaging and branding, and others dedicate their lives to helping people "find their voice" in a crazy, crowded, online market. Because of this, we'll note messaging only in the context of crowdfunding campaigns and nothing else.

For those of you who are thinking of using crowdfunding as a way to build a brand for a startup non-profit or company, I'm here to say that it is possible. If you're an artist or you are looking to raise funds for a one-time project and you think that messaging is not important, think again.

Having a consistent and clear message of who you are, what you are about, and why you need money is very important in order to be successful with your campaign. I know some of this logic may seem very elementary to most of you, but I can't stress this enough. I've seen so many campaigns that were missing one small piece of their messaging, and it caused a ripple effect throughout the rest of their campaign.

THE 10 COMMANDMENTS OF CROWDFUNDING

> **LET'S BREAK ALL OF THIS DOWN:**

- **Why are you trying to raise money?** Answering this question seems pretty self explanatory, but it is not as easy as it looks. Our society shuns the idea of sharing how much we make per hour, but in crowdfunding that gets stripped away. Tell your audience what you need the money for, and be honest. If you feel uncomfortable sharing the reason why you need the money, then don't do it. Something is holding you back, and your backers will feel it during the campaign. While you don't have to account for every single cent that comes in on your campaign, you do have to be clear about how your backer's funds will be used. Not just in the campaign video, but in the explanations on the campaign page too. Consider a pie chart showing where all expenses will go. If you can think of a fun acronym or phrase to break these expenses down, you can build it into your messaging and branding.

- **Who are you?** This is as literal as you can get. While you may want to launch a brand, get money for a project or invention, or have enough money to cover funeral expenses for a loved one, you need to share this information on your campaign page and with your backers. Gone are the days of the phrase, "Pay no attention to the man behind the curtain." You will have to think about how you relate to your campaign page personally, and then share your insights and thoughts with your backers. People know and realize that you are your own person from your campaign, and people want to see that side of you. I really thought about this when I posted this campaign update on Kickstarter:

THE 10 COMMANDMENTS OF CROWDFUNDING

Heading into the homestretch...

Good Morning Everyone!

Welcome to all of the new backers! We're into the final week of this campaign, and the exposure of the project is definitely growing. The national organization of the Lincoln Highway Association has written a letter of endorsement and support of this project, and well-known Lincoln Highway/Roadside Attraction author Brian Butko has also written a post about my journey as well, so check them out!

I'm very pleased to also report that Jon Grayson interviewed me for his Overnight America podcast yesterday, which will be broadcast nationally next week.

Despite all of this great activity, I'm still very concerned that I won't meet my goal next week. Funds raised are much lower than projected, which may put some aspects of this tour in jeopardy. The amount I came up was figuring in just venue rental fees, musician fees, insurance costs, and misc. expenses (i.e. copies of programs, occasional recordings of performances, etc.) for the listed shows on the tour schedule (roughly 20 concerts from April-September), nothing more. Again for those new to Kickstarter, this is an all-or-nothing way to raise money, so if I don't meet my goal next week, I don't get any funding. If this funding doesn't succeed on here I'll have a plan B ready, but I'm hoping I don't have to use it.

I ask that you all make a final push in getting the word out to people in your circles, especially specific people who you think would be willing to donate to this cause at any amount. I passionately believe that people should

The 10 Commandments of Crowdfunding

not have to pay to hear America's history, and this project gives people that opportunity to learn and hear something they won't read in a textbook.

Thank you all again for your contribution to this effort, and know that everything you have pledged means so much more to me than the dollar sign attached to it.

With Appreciation,

--Cece

> Again, this letter shared my progress on the campaign, but I also showed my vulnerable side in this update. People need to know you are organized, but you have to show a humanistic side to yourself as well. Show your passion and your heart to the world, and people will listen.

- **What is this really all about?** While I think we've kind of answered this question with the two preceding questions, I want to talk more in depth about your journey after the campaign. Back when I was that "early adopter," the accountability wasn't there like it is now. When people invest in a crowdfunding campaign now, they want to know that their dollars will be the seed to something bigger and possibly long-lasting. They want to know what you're up to months and years after the campaign is over, so be prepared to answer those questions the first day you launch your crowdfunding page. The more you know where you're going, the easier it will be to backtrack and be present for your backers at any given time.

THE 10 COMMANDMENTS OF CROWDFUNDING

HOW TO SAY WHAT YOU NEED TO SAY:

- **Write for your audience (i.e. backers), not for yourself.** Think about the "ideal backer": How old are they? What do they like to do in their spare time? Where do they live? Really draw an image of this backer and keep it close by when you're planning this campaign. Use the words they would use in everyday speech. The more you relate to them, the more likely you will get the dollars you need.

- **Look at the language you are using in your writing.** Is it positive? Desperate? Enjoyable? Try to stay away from words like "help," "support," or "fund," which imply you're asking for a favor rather than offering something that is desirable, an experience they're going to enjoy. Think about using phrases like, "given the chance" or "we can afford"; these phrases sound better than something like "we hope to get." You will be more successful with just a few changes of words here and there.

- **Talk to the reader.** Use "you" and "us" to create a feeling of community and sense of belonging. If I were you, I'd start using these words prior to launch as you build your community, too.

- **Keep it short and sweet.** You're competing for attention from all sorts of stimuli, as well as people reading your campaign on smartphones and tablets. Say what you've got to say in fewer words, or as I like to call it, "thumbscrolls." If it takes me too long to scroll through your page with one swipe of my thumb on my smartphone, you've lost me.

- **Craft a good conclusion to your page.** Readers tend to pay attention to the top of the page, and then they generally scroll down to the bottom. You may get a few people scanning the middle for bullet points, but all in all most people will not read your whole write-up. Make your last sentence count as much as the first.

When to Seek Outside Help with Messaging

If you just read all of this and you are still struggling with what your message is, I recommend seeking outside help before you proceed. Really sit down and figure out what is lacking, and then find the right person to talk to. I advocate talking with friends and family who have objective opinions, but if you have the means and you want your campaign to turn into a long-term business, it certainly wouldn't hurt to consult with someone who works in branding and messaging. There are all different types of people in this industry, and they will work at various rates. Shop around and see how they do his or her branding, and if you find someone who resonates with you, reach out to them.

Remember, while this project is all about something you are doing, you still have to keep your backer in mind. How will you help them with a problem they might have? What is the benefit to them by backing you? Make sure they clearly understand that before you hit that "launch" button.

The New Testament

Crowdfunding the Second Time

The 10 Commandments of Crowdfunding

THE GOSPEL OF CROWDFUNDING ACCORDING TO CECE, CHAPTER 1:
DOING MY SECOND CAMPAIGN

Like a scratching record needle, your brain is probably confused reading the title of this chapter and wondering what's happening. When I first started this book back in the fall of 2015, I had no intention of doing another crowdfunding campaign in the foreseeable future. My focus was on my music, as well as helping others with their campaigns. I would stay current with trends, continue speaking to people all over the US, and everything would be fine.

Then life happened.

My health took a sharp downward turn, and I had to spend money in places I wasn't expecting. We all can relate, I'm sure.

My plan for my next *American Songline* project in 2017-2018 is to commemorate the 100th anniversary of "The Great War" – World War I. While people typically enjoy albums that are 10-12 tracks (roughly 45-60 minutes in length), a typical song from a century ago is only 2-3 minutes long due to the recording technology of the time. This means I would likely need to double my recording production costs. Each track has to be recorded and mastered, and that takes extra time and money. Add in the extra money for rehearsals with the accompanist, as well as her time during the recording sessions.

My husband and I were looking at the costs of producing the last album, and we knew we didn't have that kind of capital to produce another one. I was really reluctant to do another crowdfunding campaign, knowing my health wasn't the best, as well as the time and work it would take to run another one.

THE 10 COMMANDMENTS OF CROWDFUNDING

But then a light bulb went off – what if I ran a flexible funding campaign to raise funds for the recording of the album? I could then keep whatever funds I raised, as well as take pre-orders for the album. While I loved working with Kickstarter and would work with them under the right circumstances, this time around I knew I had to go with Indiegogo to see how their systems work. It all became clear to me: I knew I needed to do another campaign to help bring awareness to what I was doing, and I also wanted to have the new information for this book. I could really take the lessons that I learned over the years and apply it to this one to see if my thoughts and theories truly worked.

The first thing that came to mind that I needed to work through was the campaign amount. I knew I wouldn't have to raise as much money this time as last time, and that fact immediately made me breathe a huge sigh of relief. Raising $3,000-$5,000 is much easier than $15,000. That little sliding counter would make it to its end goal faster, and because of this I know from my previous experience that people will want to contribute more. Add in the flexible funding feature that Indiegogo offers, and I felt so much better. Would I have to work just as hard on this campaign as my Kickstarter campaign? Absolutely. No dollar should be taken for granted.

The next thing I thought about was the reward tiers and what I would offer at each tier. Again, it was much easier to think of what to offer this time since there's a very tangible object at the end of this campaign: a full-length album.

- ☐ My $25 tier would definitely have a digital reward so I could maximize my return on this very common amount. A full digital album released to those backers first was the answer.

- ☐ The $10 amount would only be a partial digital album,

- ☐ The $50 would be the digital album and a physical CD mailed to his or her home (I could easily cover worldwide shipping with this tier).

- ❏ Knowing that these commonly backed tiers were covered, I could then focus on the higher tiers. Indiegogo does offer a "Featured" amount, which means when the person looks up the campaign, they will see this tier first, no matter what the amount is. I decided to make my Featured tier a $100 tier, which I have called my VIP tier. I did this to draw people in to this higher amount, in the hopes that I would meet my goal sooner.

- ❏ The other thing I really had to think about was how I could make this campaign more interactive with backers and the community-at-large. I thought about all of the sing-alongs I'd done over the years and how much people loved them, and I knew that was my next tier above the VIP tier. **They would not only be considered a VIP, they also would have the opportunity to perform with me on this new album!** I noted they could check off something on their bucket list by singing backing vocals with me on the album.

- ❏ The highest tiers above that would be limited to live performances only.

Okay, that was easy. Now what about the video? I luckily had a free 30-minute video session with a prominent video marketing coach, and she gave me a great idea for the video. I then asked friends and colleagues about the idea, and they loved it. All right, that was sorted, too.

I signed up with Indiegogo, and started playing around with it, and I noticed how easy it was. It's very intuitive, and they send you information to help you get set up, as well as tips for running a good campaign. Kickstarter provides this information on their website, but you have to search for it. Overall, this all seemed so much easier than the first time, but I'm guessing parents would say the same thing about their first child versus their second child.

This time I decided to keep a diary of my efforts so that I could share with you what happened during my campaign. I knew people would be watching me, and I felt it was important to include some behind-the-scenes information. I thought it was best to also share this information in a "real-time" sense, so you could see what I was thinking and feeling during specific times of the campaign. In turn, I hope this diary will help you get prepared for what lies ahead.

The Gospel of Crowdfunding According to Cece, Chapter 2:
Two-Week 10 Commandment Check-in

Verse 1: And Cece saw the breadth of time that had passeth, and paused to review the 10 commandments

Okay, I'm getting down to the wire with my Indiegogo campaign, and I'm taking this time to take a quick pause to check everything against the 10 Commandments from the Original Testament, and see how everything compares.

> **Commandment I:**
> **Thou shalt do extensive research on thy campaign prior to launch**

Definitely feeling good about this one. As soon as I had a feeling I was going to be doing this again, I searched for albums under "second album/CD" or "sophomore album" to see what rewards and funding goals they did, as well as how big their social media following was. It helped me confirm that my intuition about how I'd structured my rewards was correct.

I had written that timing was key earlier in the book, and I almost caught myself. I was originally going to run the campaign from May 1-30, but then I saw that May 1 is a Sunday this year, so I'm moving my launch date to May 2, which is a Monday. Phew!

While I noted that May is not the ideal month for a campaign earlier in the book, I'm hoping that the Memorial Day holiday, a celebration of veterans, will be a good tie-in to what I'm trying to raise money for.

> ## COMMANDMENT II:
> ## THOU SHALT FIND AND CREATE AN ENTHUSIASTIC COMMUNITY PRIOR TO LAUNCH

This was definitely a big plus this time around for me. Because I had been out doing the American Songline project for three years, I had a decent established following versus when I had no proof of concept with the Kickstarter campaign. Combine that with the new people I've met speaking and networking, and my targeted audience is much larger.

I also researched Facebook groups and pages related to World War I, and I joined those groups right away (some of these groups had thousands of people all over the world). Again, these groups didn't exist three years ago, so this new tool could be very instrumental to this campaign. I saw that most of these groups have a strict "no selling" policy, so I had to be strategic in how I reach out. For example, mentioning to them that I'll be working on an album of songs from the war this year, and would they have any input into the songs they'd like to hear?

I plan on posting this question this week, and I look forward to seeing what people say. I'm hoping they will express interest in wanting to pre-order the album.

I also plan on building interest in these final two weeks with personal friends and family with Facebook's new live video feature. I have not used it before, and am curious to see what results come from it.

COMMANDMENT III:
THOU SHALT PICK A PLATFORM THAT IS POPULAR AND WELL KNOWN

Done! Again, I picked Indiegogo this time for the sake of research for this book, and I will go with the flexible funding option to see how that impacts transactions once the campaign is all over.

COMMANDMENT IV:
THOU SHALT SET REALISTIC GOALS

Yes, yes, and yes. I could ask for $5,000 or more and really do it up, but I'm going to ask for $3,000 in the hopes of achieving that goal and then supersede it. One thing that I'm noting for this campaign in the hopes to achieve this goal is that for every extra $500 over the original $3,000 goal, I'll record another tune for the album. This will hopefully appeal to people who want more of this music around, plus give me the capital I need to produce this album.

COMMANDMENT V:
THOU SHALT BE CONSISTENT

So far, so good on this one. We'll be using some of the similar American Songline colors, but also adding a khaki color to symbolize the war. All of my social media pages have the same header too. In fact, I may update those headers once the campaign launches... better get working on a new cover photo for Facebook! Just another detail that you can't overlook; no details are small details when it comes to a crowdfunding campaign.

Commandment VI: Thou Shalt Have a Compelling Video on Thy Campaign Page

This has been the trickiest thing to think on and execute. I had one idea in my head, and when I bounced it off of some people, they kind of panned it. So I regrouped and then came up with an even better idea.

So when I spoke to the video consultant I mentioned earlier, she envisioned my video in a certain way. For the first minute to minute and a half, it would show me telling my story, as well as why this campaign is so important. Then, I would segue into singing a song a capella. But here's the kicker: you'd only see my face for the first phrase; you then would see other people singing along/lip syncing with me. This brings the sing-along quality to my shows onto your smartphone, plus gives it a community feel.

I originally thought about doing a flash mob near a WWI statue here in Portland, but the best example of one (there aren't many in the US – 44 to be exact), was in the middle of a traffic circle/roundabout. My friends were concerned about noise levels and parking. To create a flash mob in this area would probably not work.

I got stuck on the idea and stalled out, but then I realized this week I should use instant gratification in this world to my advantage. I will use the Facebook Live Video feature to ask my Facebook friends to submit their own smartphone video of them lip syncing/singing along with me. That way, they could do it when the spirit "moved them," and I don't have to gather a crowd around to make it happen. I will be reaching out to people tomorrow, and I hope they get their videos back to me this weekend.

The script for the video is written, and now I've got to film it.

THE 10 COMMANDMENTS OF CROWDFUNDING

> ### COMMANDMENT VII:
> ### THOU SHALT KEEP THY BACKERS ENGAGED

I'm hoping that the lip-syncing video will bring to people's attention that something's going on, but one new tool I just found out about will hopefully keep me from sending out all of those manual messages I told you about earlier in this book. One of my colleagues told me about GreenInbox.com, which is a messaging tool used for Kickstarter and Indiegogo platforms only. The fee varies, depending on how many contacts you have, but the colleague that used this for her campaign told me she got thousands of dollars from using it. I wish I would have had access to this years ago, and I'm glad I have the chance to try it out for this campaign now.

> ### COMMANDMENT VIII:
> ### THOU SHALT NOT GO IT ALONE

As I re-read that commandment's chapter, I feel a little emotional. I think about the loneliness I felt when going through the first campaign, and that loneliness bred so much frustration and sadness. I can tell you now with this second one, that has all changed. I have assigned team members to my Indiegogo campaign since I can do that, and I have people who have stepped up and noted they'd like to see the test campaign so that they can give feedback on it before it goes live. My networks and following are much stronger now, and I still feel confident that I will do well this time. I'm not feeling cocky or proud, but the support I'm feeling from friends, colleagues, mentors, and coaches is something that I can't buy from anyone.

One piece of this that is slightly different than last time is that I am enlisting a friend of mine who is in public relations (PR) to help get the word out. My husband and I wrote and designed the press release, and for a fee she will be reaching out to media nationwide to share the story. Please know that I am using this chance and her expertise not only to raise funds for the album, but to also raise awareness for next year's tour as well. I hope to get pre-orders of the CD and book gigs at the same time in one fell swoop, plus I also was genuinely curious to see if her work would, in turn, help me to advise you in this book on how to proceed with possible PR/marketing campaigns.

COMMANDMENT IX:
THOU SHALT USE SOCIAL MEDIA BEFORE, DURING, AND AFTER THE CAMPAIGN

I was definitely ready for this one!

I got some help from my team, and I wrote and scheduled my tweets in the days before it all launches. Facebook posts and campaign updates are also mapped out. My YouTube channel will have the video posted the same day the campaign launches, and I plan to update my Instagram profile as well.

COMMANDMENT X:
THOU SHALT STAY IN TOUCH WITH BACKERS AFTER THE CAMPAIGN

Obviously, I won't be able to speak on this one until the campaign is over, but I do have campaign updates in mind, including news from the recording studio as I record the album.

****

So there you have it, this is how I'm doing right now in a nutshell. As you can see, there are a lot of moving pieces that still have to come together, but all in all they are coming together nicely. Next chapter is the final week countdown – where I'll be sharing my final checklist to get ready for launch.

The Gospel of Crowdfunding According to Cece, Chapter 3:
The Day Before and the First Few Days of My Second Campaign

Verse 1: And lo, the hours flew by in those final hours before I had to hit the launch button on my campaign

But in all seriousness, the hours really did fly by. Due to a death in my family the week before, my time that final week was that much more constrained, my head scattered in a million places. I wanted to hit pause and not do this campaign, but I couldn't. Memorial Day was not going to move to a different day, and I knew if I delayed in doing this campaign it would be crowdfunding suicide.

I had my sights set on launching on Monday, May 2, so everything would line up well. That meant the final days of April were chaotic and busy to get ready for the campaign's arrival. I sent the test link of the campaign to several people in my circles, and I had a couple people take a look at the video script, too. People gave me awesome feedback about images to use, as well as clarifying my "why" in the campaign marketing copy. That helped me distill my message down to its core, and the script for the video became that much better.

The Indiegogo page didn't give any indication that my page needed to be reviewed, like my Kickstarter page was. It made me a little nervous, so I reached out to them the Friday before launch to ask if they needed to review and approve my campaign. I received a very friendly response back from an Indiegogo representative. This is what she wrote:

Janela, Apr 30, 10:02:

Hi Cecelia,

Thanks for your message! I would be happy to give you some feedback to help set your campaign up for success.

There are three key factors in creating a successful campaign:

* Tell a compelling story
* Offer perks that your audience wants
* Connect with your audience on a personal level

Fun Fact: Campaigns that send out at least three updates raise about 531% more money than those that post 2 or fewer.

I've reviewed your campaign and have three suggestions for how you can increase your chances of success:

1) Add a short summary. The very first thing you should add to your pitch, right at the very top, is a 2-3 sentence summary (in bold font) explaining what your project is about: just a quick, simple description that explains your goal, why it's so important, and why people should care. Then continue with the rest of your pitch.

2) Add more images. Consider using more images in between sections of your pitch. Illustrating parts of your story will not only help your contributors connect with what you have to say, you'll hold their attention better by breaking up big blocks of text.

Also, include images of your perks. Your contributors will want to see what they'll receive for supporting you. Be thoughtful about the images and videos you choose. You want your visual aids to make sense for the type of campaign you're running. Both style and content should support your campaign story.

Finally, try to strike a balance between your images and written text. The visual media you choose should complement your written text, but not overwhelm it.

3) Remove low-priced perks. Remove your one-dollar 'Thank You' perk. Campaigns that offer a $1 perk raise 18% less than those without. People can choose to contribute smaller amounts if they wish, but

THE 10 COMMANDMENTS OF CROWDFUNDING

having them as perk levels distracts from your other offerings. You want to highlight the best perks you have (i.e., the ones which will raise you the most funds!).

Know that once you launch your campaign, you will automatically have a pink 'Contribute Now' button where your supporters can contribute any amount they want.

If you're interested in additional resources, our Crowdfunding Field Guide is a great way to get an overview of the crowdfunding process and strategy. Strategy and outreach play a huge part in the success of a campaign, and these tools will help familiarize you with the best practices and tactics.

Additionally, I'd recommend visiting our Help Center where you can find answers to specific questions you have about crowdfunding or the more technical features on our site.

Best of luck on your campaign, and please let us know if we can help with anything else!

Cheers,

Janela
Customer Happiness

All great tips! I couldn't add images to my rewards for some reason, but I took her advice and did everything else. It was clear that I didn't have to get approval for my campaign, so all we had to do was get the video ready.

I gave everyone until noon Sunday to turn in his or her lip-synced videos for the crowdfunding video, and then on Sunday afternoon it was go time. Dan and I filmed my portion of the video, and then we started the editing process.

THE 10 COMMANDMENTS OF CROWDFUNDING

BEHIND THE SCENES VIDEO SETUP

For a two-to-three-minute video, it took us from start to finish about six hours to make the final product you now see on YouTube and on the Indiegogo page. And this was not our first rodeo with doing a crowdfunding video. If it's your first time, allow at least a day's work, maybe two to get everything ready.

Everything else was put on hold, and we ate whatever semi-healthy takeout food we could get our hands on. My PR friend helping me advised me to create a Facebook event for the campaign so that people who weren't my friends could be invited to the event page, and therefore could learn more about the campaign and share or back it. I created a draft event, but did not make it live. That would have to wait until morning.

The 10 Commandments of Crowdfunding

Verse 2: Yea, and the day of the campaign launch arriveth. Excitement abounded in my heart for the whole day, but there were some obstacles to overcome.

Sleep was elusive the night before. My mind kept me up thinking about all of the things I needed to do on launch day. Did I forget anything? "Okay, after I hit launch, then I have to email this person, then this person, then this other person…" It went on and on.

I finally just got up at 5:30 in the morning, and took a few quiet moments to pause and get ready for what was coming. My body remembered feeling this way three years ago, so while I was nervous, I still felt as good as I was going to feel about it all.

At 6 am Pacific time on Monday, May 2, 2016, I hit the "review and launch" button and one final screen popped up verifying all of the things that I could not change once I launched. Yes, I wanted to do flexible funding, and for the $3,000 amount. I hit launch, and it went live. The screen had a dashboard at the top of the screen to help me keep track of everything, and I knew there was no turning back.

I then made the Facebook event link live, and started to invite people left and right. I hit my 500-person limit, hit "invite," and then everything stopped. Facebook notified me that I invited people "too fast" and that I'd been blocked from inviting people to my own event.

I freaked out, and then I panicked. I reached out to a few friends who know many of my mutual friends and let them know what was happening. I shared the event link with them, and within an hour hundreds of people had been invited. Phew! This is where the "Thou Shalt Not Go It Alone" commandment is extremely important.

I then started updating all of my social media pages to show the new cover photos that tie in with the campaign. I also published a new blog post I had drafted the night before, and then I reached out to my Kickstarter backers with an update to let them know what had been going on with me. After that, I started sending out emails to my crowdfunding list and American Songline list, tailoring my emails to my audience.

Amongst all of this, the donations started rolling in. I received an email notification every time it happened, with the amount and the rewards (if any) claimed. It felt good to see that people were seeing my campaign and backing it. People also started sharing the campaign link on Facebook and Twitter, and that was huge for me.

I was talking with a colleague who has crowdfunded before, and she and I were commenting about how people feel like they somehow can't share your campaign via social media if they are not able to donate money to it. That is just crazy! I'm telling you all now, please let your audiences know that sharing and commenting on a campaign is extremely important and crucial to its success, whether or not they donate. While I'd love all of the dollars for my campaign to appear in the first 24 hours, I know that's not realistic. Having 10, 20, even 30 people share, like, and comment on your campaign in those first few days is so important to the campaign's success. The more people that see it, the more likely people will donate.

Between the social media, emails, and launching, I put in a 12-hour day on launch day. I was tired when everything was said and done, but it was all worth it. Ten percent of the target funds were raised this day.

VERSE 3: AND WEARY WAS THE CROWDFUNDER ON THE SECOND AND THIRD DAYS OF THE CAMPAIGN; BUT SHE HAD TO KEEP GOING.

Day two I was extremely tired from the previous day, but the donations were still coming in, which was awesome. I was suddenly able to invite and post on the event Facebook page; again more progress.

One thing that also really started to come in were the messages from crowdfunding consultants, PR, and social media people who said they could help me with my campaign. The only way Indiegogo allows me to reply to anyone (if I wanted to reply back to those solicitors) was to reply back through their system and give them my email address to contact me again. This is definitely a drawback with Indiegogo versus Kickstarter. Kickstarter has an independent messaging system within their website, so all exchanges happen through their site. Because of this, I never got spammed as badly as I did with Indiegogo. I also feel I got fewer messages because people just weren't interested in crowdfunding three years ago. It saddens me that there's so much of it out there.

Tuesday afternoon I crashed. Hard. I did a podcast interview and accountability coaching call before 2 pm along with everything else; I didn't feel like doing anything other than sitting in my rocker/recliner and watch TV. I paused and rested for the rest of the day.

Day 3 I knew I had to keep up momentum, so I emailed a bunch of people with the link letting them know the campaign was live, and I also did some more live video on social media and shared those. The Facebook event on both those days was still causing confusion for those invited. People thought it was a live performance, and then people were getting annoyed that it was two weeks long (the longest amount of time an event can be on Facebook). Because I could no longer change the dates, I decided to delete the old event and replace it with a new event that had only the end date of the campaign. I noted in several places that it was an online event, and that it was an ongoing, active event for the whole month of May. I slowly started inviting people to the event, and things started to pick up. Lesson learned!

Donations came in slowly on this day, but not as much as I expected. I chalked it up to the beginning of the month. When I did my Kickstarter campaign, I launched in the middle part of the month, and a lot of donations came in really quickly. Then I hit the dreaded plateau around the middle of the campaign (near the first of the next month). Now older and wiser, I think the dreaded plateau was because everyone had to pay rent at that time.

Because of this, I've decided to do my mass messaging via Green Inbox during the second and third weeks of the campaign when people will hopefully be able to back me. I'll do Facebook one week, and LinkedIn the following week.

When I logged into my Indiegogo dashboard tonight, I saw this:

> **Introducing a new way to boost your fundraising**
> This month we're debuting a pilot program designed to put more fundraising power in the hands of entrepreneurs and campaign organizers like yourself. Program participants will have the opportunity both to keep a larger share of funds raised and to access extra marketing support from the Indiegogo team. We'll be in touch within 24 hours if your campaign qualifies!

To no surprise to anyone reading this, I hit "I'm interested," and they told me they would notify me if I were chosen. I do really hope I'm chosen; I'm very intrigued by the possibilities that this program could present. Fingers crossed!

The Gospel of Crowdfunding According to Cece, Chapter 4:
The End of the First Week of My Second Campaign

Verse 1: Days four and five cometh and goeth, and a stillness came across the land.

These past couple days have been fairly quiet, more behind-the-scenes-like in regards to keeping momentum up. On Day 4, I posted a more formal post to all of the World War I groups I belong to, noting the following:

Hello everyone,

As some of you know, I am a classically trained musician who specializes in performing music from the early part of the 20th Century. For my next album I'll be recording music from the World War I era, sung with full verses and choruses the way they were meant to be heard. I'm in the process of raising funds for the studio production costs to record these songs, and the more funds I raise, the more music I can preserve for future generations to hear.

If you can donate to the Indiegogo campaign anytime this in May, you'll receive this music before it's released to the general public. If you are not able to donate during the month, would you mind sharing this with people who might be interested in knowing more about it? Every dollar and new contact helps me reach my goal. Thanks again, and if I can ever help YOU, just say the word. https://igg.me/at/songsofWWI.

So far, there's activity from it, but no donations as of yet. I don't want to be a hard sell in these groups, because if I am I may get kicked out. I am curious to see what comes of using these groups, and if they are truly a valuable tool for campaigns.

Another podcast interview with *The Weird History Podcast* also went live, and that interview directly mentions the campaign. No donations as of yet, but again, it's early.

I also wrote several organizations and people via email about what I was doing, and that did produce one $100 donation. Not too shabby. Some of my good friends also reposted the campaign or the Facebook event page link that Thursday evening and one of them noted:

> "If just half of my Facebook friends contributed just $5, she'd be completely funded!"

Another friend wrote:

> "Every dollar you give creates time travel! How cool is that?"

By the time Day 5 came (Friday), I knew it was time to give people an update on Facebook and thank backers for their support. Mother's Day was that weekend, so most people were not going to be near their computers. Here's what I wrote:

Less than a week into the Indiegogo campaign, and we're at 21%! Special thanks go out to the following backers, Facebook sharers and awesome get-the-word out people: [names and Facebook pages inserted here]. Thank you all for your help, I couldn't have done it without you!

If you haven't seen or shared the campaign yet, you can check it out at this link: https://igg.me/at/songsofWWI. If ALL of my 750+ Facebook friends gave a minimum of $5-10 to *this campaign, I'd be fully funded immediately, and this music would be preserved for generations to come. Rewards start at $10, but any amount helps. You'll also get first access to everything before the public does.*

Again, thank you all for your support this week and in the coming weeks, and if there's ever anything I can do for you please ask!

While I only have 13 backers as I write this, I thought it was a good thing to give shout-outs to those who have been sharing the campaign on their personal and business pages. What they do matters, and they should be given recognition. Plus, it also creates more tagged names in the post, and that means more people see it.

Verse 2: The stillness persisted throughout the Sabbath, but I remained hopeful for what was yet to come.

Saturday (Day 6) of the first campaign week was pretty uneventful. I did get two more backers in the last 24 hours, so I'm now up to 15 backers and $800, which means 27% of my $3,000 goal is now officially met. I anticipated this weekend being quiet because it's Mother's Day. People would be spending money on their moms and spending time with their families, so I didn't want to post about the campaign. It just seemed in poor taste to be promoting something for such an emotionally charged time for people.

My curiosity was getting the best of me, so I thought I'd compare my first campaign with the current one to see if there were any similarities/differences so far. Here are the stats for the first week:

The 10 Commandments of Crowdfunding

	Kickstarter (2013)	Indiegogo (2016)
Number of backers for the first week	19	15
Funds Raised	$845 – 5% of total goal for the campaign	$800 – 27% of goal for the total campaign

Keep in mind, my first campaign had a higher end goal, so the numbers are slightly skewed from that perspective. One thing that I will say that is on my side this time is the overall social reach I have versus the first campaign. More Facebook friends, more advocates, and more support have made things go much better this first week versus the first campaign. I have the feeling these two campaigns will take two different tracks, but only time will tell in the coming weeks.

The Gospel of Crowdfunding According to Cece, Chapter 5:
The Second Week

Verse 1: And I entered into the second week of the campaign, which began more like a lamb, not a lion.

It's been pretty quiet here the last couple days, but backers continue to trickle in and give. People have contributed every day to this campaign since it launched, except on Mother's Day, which is really great. It's much more reassuring to have this happen than to have no one contribute for days at a time (which happened in 2013). At the moment, I'm at 29% funded, and between all of the social media and behind-the-scenes email, I think things are starting to pay off.

My social community at large has been active in sharing it on Facebook over the last couple days, which has really upped the video and campaign page views. It goes to show people are really behind this and trying to support me in any way they can. Here are more things I did this week:

- Another update to my 2013 Kickstarter backers linking to the video, and another plea for them to support this project.
- Another Facebook live video on Tuesday, and that video resulted in another contribution. In that video I noted my progress, as well as telling people that rewards started at $10 (the price of two lattes). I also noted that I'd be sharing

The 10 Commandments of Crowdfunding

special updates with backers only, so if they wanted to hear and see those updates I recommended that they contribute to see them.

My PR person started sharing the campaign and reaching out to media contacts, and so far nothing yet. In our conversations she noted to add more hashtags to all of my posts. I was doing 1-2, and she suggested five key ones for Facebook. I'm working with about ten different hashtags on Twitter and Instagram, but will use the top five for Facebook.

I rehearsed with my piano accompanist the day after Mother's Day, and I recorded some of our rehearsal. I thought it would be nice to give backers a sneak peek into what things will sound like. When I went to post a campaign update, I saw that I couldn't upload an MP3 music file into the update (only text, images, or video). I contacted Indiegogo support, and asked how I can add this type of file to an update. The same rep I had last time contacted me, and she noted that I could not add this type of file directly; I had to add it to Dropbox (an outside file sharing service) and share the link from Dropbox for the update.

This is *very* different from Kickstarter, as they will let you share audio directly to your campaign page. I wrote my Indiegogo person and told her that they should consider doing this for the future, as their competitors have this capability. I realize it's not important for some of you, but if you are a musician reading this you should note that accordingly. I wrote and posted the update, and it was a quick and easy process.

Verse 2: Lo, the community gathered around, and gave encouraging words and contributions of support to the crowdfunder. The crowdfunder was still weary, but very hopeful she would succeed before the campaign was finished.

I can't believe it's only been nine days. Like with anything important one does, the time has flown and dragged at the same time. A few more contributions came in today so far, and I'm now at 34% funded with 23 backers as I write this. Again, I'd of course like to be fully funded right now so I could get a full night's sleep, but overall I'm pleased with the progress thus far. Unlike three years ago, people in my social circles really understand now that sharing the campaign helps so much in giving it staying power. I also think the topic has a good universal appeal as well, so people really understand more about what I'm doing and can therefore promote it better.

While I was in the process of writing this book in the winter of 2016, a friend and colleague of mine was telling me about a tool she used on her 2015 Kickstarter campaign. The tool was called Green Inbox, and through this tool she was able to get thousands of dollars with minimal effort. Intrigued, I looked into it.

Green Inbox was developed after my 2013 campaign, hence why I had never heard of it before. They work with Indiegogo and Kickstarter campaigns only, so if you are thinking of using another platform, this won't work with it.

You create a message that's 600 characters or less, and then they send an email or message on your behalf to various friends and connections on social media for just pennies per message. Because of those tricky social media algorithms I keep talking about, this is a low-cost way to get an email message to everyone quickly that you could guarantee would be seen. Wanting to save myself some time and money, as well as give you a secret insider trick, I took a chance and signed up for it.

I wanted to time my private messages via Green Inbox so that it was in the middle of the second week – far enough from Mother's Day, but close enough to everyone's next paycheck. Plus this would also be timed during the dreaded plateau I spoke about earlier. When I was reviewing everything before signing up with them, I saw they offered a full money-back guarantee if I did not get a certain amount of contributions. In order to get this guarantee, I had to email them for a coupon code. They got back to me with the coupon code, and I set everything up. Please note that to use their service it does take them 24-48 hours to get those messages into your friends' inboxes, so don't use them if you are toward the end of your campaign (they also caution against this).

Because of the fatigue, I felt like some kind of cold virus or something wanted to come and wreak havoc on my immune system. To protect myself, I had to cancel some get-togethers with friends so I could keep my sanity. I found it hard to do this, but again, this campaign is only temporary and I'm hoping my friends understand. I have looked at my calendar for the rest of the month, and I'm restricting myself to outings that could affect the bottom line of my campaign (i.e. performances, networking, and mastermind groups where people know me and what I'm doing).

I've been eating on the run or barely at all, so I'm also making sure I eat as healthy as I can with minimal effort. Our slow cooker has been running more than usual, but this is great, as it allows for meals to be cooked at home with little effort. Also, having leftovers is a plus. I remember feeling all of this three years ago, and wished that I didn't feel this way again. But, the energy to undertake something like this is no small feat, no matter how old you are.

The Gospel of Crowdfunding According to Cece, Chapter 6:
The Sequel to the Second Week

Verse 1: And Cece stretcheth out her hand toward the rocky contributionless crowdfunding sea, and Green Inbox maketh the sea become dry ground, and the clear path made the Indiegogo campaign gain strong momentum toward the promised land.

The last couple of days have been nuts. Absolutely nuts. When Green Inbox notified me that they'd send out two waves of emails to my Facebook friends (one batch Thursday, and one Friday), I had no idea how crazy it would get. The first 350 emails went out, and within hours I had made back my small investment and then some. I had gone from 34% funding/23 backers before Green Inbox to 49%/35 backers within 36 hours. That's mind-blowing to me compared to my first campaign when there were long periods of nothing. I also had a lot of people write me after they got their emails to say they couldn't donate at this time, but they would share the campaign with people that they know. Again, that's huge. Any interaction is a good interaction, and that's what Green Inbox helped me with in a short amount of time.

The second wave went out on Friday, and it wasn't as dramatic as Thursday's wave. I had people contacting me, but due to the impending weekend the donations steadily came in. By late Friday night, I had 50% funding. In only 11 days!

THE 10 COMMANDMENTS OF CROWDFUNDING

I woke up the next morning, and the contributions were still coming in, and I was now at 53%. People were remarking that they knew about the campaign, but they appreciated the email reminder. Phew! I was glad to hear that – I was really worried about annoying people.

Once I knew we had crossed this threshold, I posted an update to all the backers first, and then did a Facebook Live video on my American Songline page noting the link and appropriate hashtags. I re-shared that video to my personal page, and then tagged everyone who gave this past week and thanked them. People started sharing that video, and the contributions and emails kept coming in.

I had a few more emails from people noting they were watching the campaign, and would contribute later in the month due to finances. I also had a friend and former teacher email me and tell me that she wanted to contribute, but wanted to do so via check due to Internet fraud from another campaign she backed in the past. I noted my mailing address in the email, and let my spouse know about the contribution so we could be in the lookout for it.

By the time I reached the end of Day 14 (the third Monday of the campaign), I was 69% funded, and I had 46 backers. Not too shabby for less than halfway through! People were still contributing and writing me from the Green Inbox emails I sent. I did more updates to the backers and via social media on this day, and kind of crashed from it all.

I know I've talked about this in previous chapters in the book, but before you launch the campaign, make sure you have things in place that will help you deal with the stress accordingly. Allow yourself to take breaks, and remember your schedule will shift during this time. I'm not a couple weeks into this campaign, and I swear my body "remembers" what this feels like. I'm tired all of the time, my brain is all over the place, I'm hungry way more than I normally am, and at times I can feel my body holding my head and neck in a tense position. It's crazy how much I'm noticing this time, but it's also interesting to note that it's happening. While it all feels familiar, stress is still stress.

THE 10 COMMANDMENTS OF CROWDFUNDING

I'm very grateful that I work from home and can adapt my schedule as I need to, but if I had a regular 9-5 job it would be impossible to manage all of this. I think if I had that type of job while running a campaign, I'd build time off into my schedule prior to launch to stay on task with the campaign, as well as to relax from it all. Having healthy snacks on hand is crucial – while I do feel fatigued I felt better eating foods at home and not living off of takeout.

Remember, people will be contacting you at all hours of the day, and you need to be at your best to engage them and answer your questions. If you aren't at your best, this can influence so many things with your campaign, including your bottom line.

The halfway point is coming soon, and I'm feeling better on some levels about this campaign versus my first one. The steady support of social media and contributions has made this campaign feel less crazed. But keep in mind: it is not over until it's over!

THE 10 COMMANDMENTS OF CROWDFUNDING

The Gospel of Crowdfunding According to Cece, Chapter 7:
The Halfway Point and Observations from the Third Week

Verse 1: Day 15 of the 30-day campaign arriveth, and the crowdfunder continued her quest for funding through any electronic means necessary.

Compared to other days on the campaign so far, it was quieter on Day 15 than other days. I put in my order with Green Inbox for them to send emails to my LinkedIn contacts in the morning, and selected everyone I hadn't heard from yet. It came to $29.80, and I anticipated those emails going out later this week. I did some more posting on social media, noting it was the halfway point in the campaign, did the appropriate hashtags, and posted it. My friend in PR did a posting too, and those posts received a lot of likes and shares.

I did an email blast to my list as well, thanking them for everything so far, and not too long after that I received three contributions. That put the funding at 72%. I spoke on the phone with a fellow crowdfunder to check in and strategize, and it really helped me confirm my intuition about how to do everything in the final 15 days. Since I'm was in a good place funding wise, I just needed to keep applying a steady pressure of email, social media, and reaching out to Facebook groups.

THE 10 COMMANDMENTS OF CROWDFUNDING

VERSE 2: THE THIRD WEEK CONTINUED ON, AND YEA, THE CROWDFUNDER RAN INTO DIFFICULTIES WITH LINKEDIN.

The first wave of emails to my LinkedIn contacts went out with Green Inbox earlier than expected, approximately 24 hours after I placed the order. Unlike Facebook, I received a bunch of returned emails – almost 30 defunct email addresses. Some of my LinkedIn contacts did donate, but I had more people who were not able to contribute and people who were not interested in contributing. I had more people who noted they would share this with people and get the word out, to which I replied back and heartily thanked them. Again, the more people who see the campaign, the better it will get funded. I loved hearing from people I haven't heard from in a while, and it gave me a chance to reconnect with them, too.

On Day 17, I surpassed 75% funding, and did a campaign update to all backers, as well as some general social media posts. I did two networking events that day, and I had a really hard time leaving the house and being away from the computer. I didn't feel totally 100%, but I knew I needed to do those events to further this campaign, as well as thank people in person who had donated. It ended up being really good for me, as I found new contacts to talk to about the project, as well as remind people who knew me to donate. I left the events hoping it would pay off soon.

The Gospel of Crowdfunding According to Cece, Chapter 8:
The Final 10 Days of the Campaign

Verse 1: The twentieth day of the campaign arriveth, and yea, the goal was in sight. The crowdfunder was crossing her fingers, hoping for 100% funding soon.

While the campaign had excellent momentum during Days 18-20, personally they were difficult days for me. The morning of Day 18 started off well – I did another podcast interview, and more contributions came in. But then, life happened.

At lunchtime I happened to glance down at my almost 18-year old cat, and noticed she was not putting weight on one of her legs. In fact, she was barely walking at all. Knowing that she is not young anymore and we had never seen her like this ever, we immediately dropped everything, I cancelled the rest of my appointments that day, and went straight to the emergency veterinarian.

They x-rayed her, and by a stroke of luck, nothing was broken. They did notice the soft tissue around one of her ankles was swollen, and they thought she must have landed on it wrong. They noted this cat (almost 89 in human years) would heal from her injury in a few days with rest and pain medication, and if not, we should contact them immediately. I was relieved it wasn't something worse, but I still felt bad for her.

Physically and emotionally, I was officially a wreck. We had to take care of this cat, and we were worried that she could injure herself more in the healing process. I did minimal maintenance with the campaign (I did check in on social media, thanking people, answering emails), but that's it. No Facebook live videos, no newsletters, nothing else. I have to say, if I didn't have Green Inbox helping me during the campaign, I would have really struggled to keep going. It would have been hard to stay motivated in the campaign if I had the busywork of manually emailing people like I did three years ago. On top of everything, I had a studio recital performance in a couple of days, and I wasn't even sure if I was going to go, depending on how the cat was feeling.

She healed pretty well, and I decided to sing at the performance, even though I was exhausted. I didn't really feel up to going, but I knew video from this performance would help the campaign, as well as the overall project. I got up and did a couple of songs from the prospective World War I program, and people *loved* it. It was clear I was on the right path with all of this, and having that feedback cemented it more.

Day 20 was finally upon me, and all I kept thinking was, "I want this campaign to be over!" Like a woman in the final trimester of her pregnancy, I was excited about what was to come, but I was so worn out. Memorial Day weekend was almost upon us, and I wanted to reach my goal before the weekend, since I knew people would be away from their computers.

On a personal level, I also was frustrated with the lack of support from family at this time. These two campaigns I've done are both like children to me, and the fact that some family members didn't acknowledge those children was difficult. Other crowdfunding experts have noted in other webinars and articles to never count on your friends and family for financial support during a campaign, and I wholeheartedly agree. I think families will be there for you when the chips are down, but if you're expecting them to fund your campaign you will be sorely mistaken. You try not to let it get to you, but it's hard to have to face that reality.

THE 10 COMMANDMENTS OF CROWDFUNDING

VERSE 2: "WE WENT THROUGH FIRE AND THROUGH WATER, YET YOU BROUGHT US OUT INTO A PLACE OF ABUNDANCE." (PSALM 66:12)

As a person currently living in Pacific Time Zone, I find it fascinating how much of the world lives their lives hours ahead of me. We are one of the last groups of people to ring in the New Year, and every night I watch as my social media feeds slowly quiet down and "go to bed." Sometimes if I am up late, I can catch my friends' morning posts from Ireland.

What did this mean for this campaign and for me? It meant I would wake up to a world already in action, with contributions coming in, and people tweeting and sharing what I do with the world long before I eat breakfast.

On the morning of Day 21, I wrote this update to all of my backers:

> As Day 21 was turning into Day 22 (Indiegogo's calendar runs on 24 hour blocks), this campaign was also 100% funded at the exact same time. Needless to say, there were various cheers and happy dances done around the house when that moment happened, and I have to admit I'm still in awe from it all.
>
> This album is so much more than just music to me; it's a chance to tell the stories of those who have long since left this Earth. A time period that gets lost in the cracks of the Internet often, yet this period in history has shaped and continues to shape all that we are as people today. It is an absolute honor to be able to now preserve these songs for future generations, and I am forever grateful to all of

THE 10 COMMANDMENTS OF CROWDFUNDING

you who decided to support me and take this journey.

Now, you're probably thinking, "What happens next?" While the campaign is 100% funded, the campaign does not end until 11:59 pm PST on June 1st (8 more days). This means that I am still able to accept donations and pre-orders on the album, so keep sharing this project with anyone and everyone you know who will appreciate it. Remember, for every extra $500 donated above the campaign goal, I will record another song for the album. At $1,000, two songs. And so forth and so on. People are actually more likely to back the campaign now that it's fully funded, so you can assure anyone you talk to that this project will definitely happen.

Stay tuned for more posts, videos, and songs; again thank you all for everything and let's keep the momentum going!

I also did a Facebook Live video, and I remarked that I felt like "Miss America," and it was true. I could feel myself trying not to cry tears of happiness from it all. I also felt a *huge* sense of relief. My original goal had been met days before the holiday weekend, and I knew I could sleep better knowing I had given it my all and it had paid off. I knew I didn't have to do any big pushes or email campaigns, I just had to keep up a steady presence online, be ready to answer people's emails, and remain in a happy, grateful, and humble mind frame.

I woke up the next day and took it easy. I went out for a couple of hours in the evening and had fun with my friends. The campaign had changed in the last 24 hours, and while I felt the need to see if could meet my stretch goal, it wasn't all weighing on my mind as it was before.

With the flexible funding Indiegogo option, it appeared that the money was immediately taken out of people's accounts when they backed the campaign, which is completely the opposite of Kickstarter. With Kickstarter's model, there's another added risk. They not only work on an all-or-nothing platform, but people's contributions don't come out until the campaign is over. This means people have the time to change their mind about their pledge; they can increase or decrease their bid as much as they want before the campaign is over. I did not have anyone retract their pledges with my Kickstarter campaign, but I have heard of this happening to others in the 11th hour of a campaign, and in turn they almost lost everything. On a lightly related note, I thought it was interesting that Kickstarter's clock counts down, while Indiegogo's counts up. This means I had an extra day, which was nice.

Right around the one-week remaining mark, I got this message on my dashboard:

Looking good there!

Starting today your campaign page has a shiny new look. Building on feedback from campaigners and backers alike, we've made some changes to help you share your story with the largest possible audience.

Connect better with backers on any device
Your campaign is now easier to browse (and back!) on mobile, tablet, and desktop.

More contributions, higher engagement
The results are in: With the new design in place, more visitors are backing and sharing your campaign.

A turbo boost for your campaign
The new design loads twice as fast, which means more eyes on your campaign.

Keep your eyes out in the coming weeks as we continue to roll out features that help you share your story and hit your goals.

THE 10 COMMANDMENTS OF CROWDFUNDING

I did like the changes that were made; the page now looks fantastic on mobile devices, as you can see by the screenshot below:

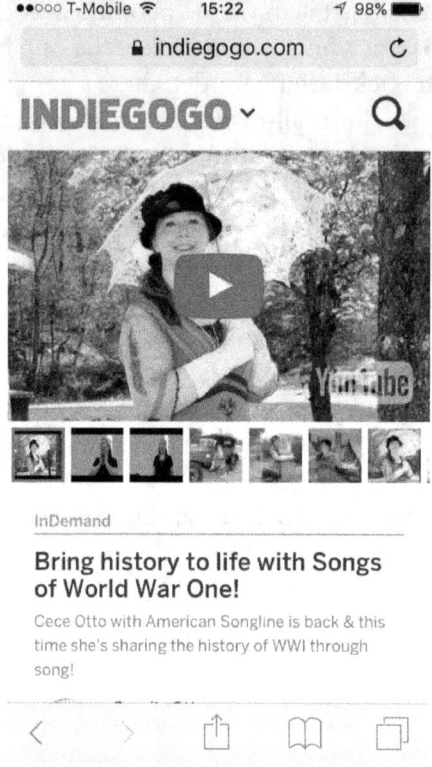

Contributions still kept coming in, and before I knew, it was the Friday before Memorial Day. I knew I had to stay fresh in the minds of everyone before they went out of town or offline, so I did a special backer update with a video from last week's studio performance, noting the statistics of the lives lost in World War I. I noticed a bunch of contributions came in on that Friday, and I'm guessing it was because many people got paid and had the disposable income to help out. With their contributions, I was almost halfway to my stretch goal!

Verse 3: The weekend of remembrance came upon the land, and whilst a holiday calm was present, the people were not silent about thy crowdfunding campaign.

The final days of the campaign were here! I refrained from posting on social media about the campaign for the weekend, sticking with topics about Memorial Day itself. On Sunday, I sent out a newsletter to my list sharing my personal thoughts on the day, as well as giving them a campaign update. Believe it or not, I had a few contributions come in that day and on Memorial Day because of it.

Tuesday morning I woke up to more contributions, which got me over my stretch goal, and then some! I did another update to all backers, and using clever photos and memes, I put up posts on social media to remind people that the campaign was coming to an end. On my personal page, I posted a 24-hour reminder meme before I went to bed that night, and I went back and tagged anyone and everyone who backed, contributed to social media, or gave me words of encouragement. I didn't even focus on the dollar amount; all I focused on was the number of backers. I had 97 backers when I posted to Facebook, and I told people it would be awesome to have 100 backers when everything was over.

On the final day, the contributions continued to roll in, as well as the social media shares. I stayed up until the end of the campaign, and here's what the screen shots looked like as it turned over:

THE 10 COMMANDMENTS OF CROWDFUNDING

Bring history to life with Songs of World War One!

Cece Otto with American Songline is back & this time she's sharing the history of WWI through song!

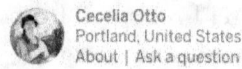
Cecelia Otto
Portland, United States
About | Ask a question

$3,845 USD raised by 102 backers

128% of $3,000 flexible goal   a minute left

I wrote these words after midnight, and I couldn't believe it was over. I watched those final minutes slip away, and it started to wash over me how this was all coming to a glorious end. It was a lot of hard work, but for me, it was worth it on so many levels.

What this second campaign really confirmed for me was:

1. You need to have your community in place ready to go before you launch. If that's not ready, wait. And then wait some more.

2. Timing is everything. From running a campaign around a topic that's timely to choosing when to launch a campaign, you need to think about those timings and plan strategies around the lulls.

3. Find a variety of ways to engage your audience that you will enjoy doing. If you don't enjoy reaching out to people about who you are and what you're trying to raise money for through crowdfunding, then rethink your strategies before you launch.

4. Keep momentum steady. Doing something every day will make an impact on your bottom line. Out of the entire campaign, there were only three days that I didn't receive online contributions. They were: 1) Mother's Day (no big shocker there); 2) The day after the campaign was 100% funded (BUT received a check in the mail from one of my high school teachers); 3) The Saturday before Memorial Day (BUT received a cash donation). I made it a game with myself to see if I could get at least one backer a day, and as far as I'm concerned I was pretty much successful at it. Contributions are contributions no matter how they arrived, and I took it as a sign from the universe to keep going.

5. No matter how many ways I thought a person would see what I was up to, I still had people who only saw it through one source, whether that was Facebook, email, or other social media outlets. Diversify your reach, and people will eventually hear you.

6. Encourage people who can't donate to share on social media networks, and then share some more. As noted earlier, I think there are a lot of people who really thought and believed that they couldn't share the campaign because they didn't donate to it. Please tell them it's okay; their shares are just as valuable as contributions sometimes, for it keeps the momentum alive, and brings people to the project who might not otherwise be engaged.

7. Only use PR if you've got a friend that will do it for you, is passionate about the campaign, and they will do it for free or cheaply (i.e. $500 or less). I personally didn't see much difference in the results that came my way using a PR person this time, and again, your community is who you need to care about most.

8. I could have made my goal $5,000, but after doing my research on other albums I went with $3,000 and ended up getting around $4,000 in those 30 days. Again, be realistic

The 10 Commandments of Crowdfunding

about how much funds you will raise for what you are doing.

9. Find affordable tools like Green Inbox to maximize your time running your campaign, versus just doing busy work. The small fee they charge is worth it, trust me!

10. Last but not least, don't think about how you "could have done x, y, or z." I kept wondering toward the end if I had done enough, but the truth is I did do enough. I planned before launch knowing what to expect, and if you do the same you will be okay. I promise. ☺

Appendix

When I was in the early stages of writing this book, I was asked as a campaign creator to participate in a university survey about crowdfunding. Early results have been published, and I have been given permission by the professor of this study to cite this work in this book. This abstract is more technical, so if you're not interested in this you can skip this section. As in the Prologue, I will note comments below each main question/statement, this time in italics so you can see my thoughts on this data.

Benchmarks from the Wharton Crowdfunding Study

Professor Mollick is the Assistant Professor of Management, and also an Edward B. and Shirley R. Shils Assistant Professor.

Mollick, Ethan (2016). Benchmarks from the Wharton Crowdfunding Study. Retrieved from https://crowdfunding.wharton.upenn.edu/.

Methodology

For the creator survey: A stratified sample of 65,326 Kickstarter project creators were surveyed via email. Of those projects, 10,493 completed part of the survey (16%) and 7,788 (12%) completed the entire survey, these response rates are comparable with other web-based surveys in non-traditional industries. Response rates varied by amount pledged with larger projects responding at a higher rate. After controlling for this factor, there was no significant difference between respondents and non-respondents in number of experienced backers, number of novice backers, number of other projects backed by the creator on Kickstarter, or in the number of serial projects by the creator.

This was the survey I participated in, and I have to say I thought the survey was pretty easy to complete. I'm a little surprised to see people didn't complete the survey in full.

For the backer survey: In total 456,751 backers were surveyed, representing 65,326 projects. All projects from 2009 through May 2015 that raised over $1,000 were included in the sample, as well as half the projects that raised less than $1,000 but over $250, and a quarter of projects raising less than $250. Backers were selected randomly, without replacement, to maximize the number of backers per project. A mean of 7.2 backers were surveyed per project, with 7 backers surveyed in 89% of projects and 10 backers surveyed in 7.8% of projects. A total of 47,188 backers (10.3%) responded. In total, there is at least one response for 30,323 projects (46.4% of all projects), with 1.56 backer responses per project on average.

I had no idea a backer survey was conducted during this research, so seeing this information on the early publication was a pleasant surprise.

WHY DO PEOPLE REALLY BACK PROJECTS?

Based on my survey of backers, the two most popular reasons why people back projects is because they either want to support the creator or they want to support the vision behind the project. Backing projects because of the reward is a distant third.

I completely concur with these findings, and have seen this time and time again in my own campaign, as well as in other campaigns.

The 10 Commandments of Crowdfunding

How do you make backers of one of your projects likely to back you again?

I ran a number of statistical models to try to discover what factors led backers to say that they would be willing to back a project creator again. These models controlled for factors like the project category, funds raised, and goal size.

First, I discovered, perhaps unsurprisingly, that campaigns that deliver on their promise are associated with having backers that are more likely to back creators again. Backers who thought that creators communicated about changes to the project were also significantly more likely to back the creators again, even if the project changed direction by a large amount. Interestingly, the number of Kickstarter updates only had a small effect on the backer's perception of communication – update quality seems to matter more than the number of updates. Backers were also more likely to back creators again if they thought the project outcome was innovative.

Most other factors – including the prior experience of the project creators in running projects (which included factors like budgeting, organizing, working with suppliers, etc.), did significantly not impact the willingness of backers to back projects again.

Most of this information does not surprise me. I think the line that jumps out at me most was that "update quality seems to matter more than the number of updates." This is very important to think about when planning a campaign. This data would then suggest all the more that your updates count, and don't throw things up in a willy-nilly fashion.

Why do successful creators launch projects?

While money is an important reason for seeking Kickstarter funds, it is only one of the goals for most projects. The most popular reasons, in order, were: "to generate awareness for my project," "the project could not have been funded without the money from Kickstarter," and "to connect directly with a community of my fans or supporters."

I again agree with the reasons and their order on this question. For both of my projects, that's pretty much how my answers fell.

HOW MUCH TIME DO SUCCESSFUL CREATORS SPEND ON THEIR PROJECTS?

Just over 2/3 of projects were launched by individuals, and the other 1/3 by teams. Launching and running a project was an involved process, and the hours did not vary much between the pre-campaign setup, the campaign itself, and the fulfillment of the campaign.

- Average amount of hours spent per week setting up the campaign: 30
- Average amount of hours spent per week the campaign is running: 31
- Average amount of hours spent per week once the campaign is over: 31

Interesting to see how many campaigns were run by an individual versus teams. The hours spent working on a campaign before, during, and after was about the same, which from experience doesn't surprise me. But as you can see, 30 hours a week is no small amount of your time. As noted before, treat this campaign like another full-time job.

WHAT ARE THE MOST COMMON CAUSES OF PROJECT DELAYS?

I asked those who said that their project was delayed about the reasons. Working with partners (like suppliers and manufacturers) was the most common reason for delay, followed by fulfillment.

The 10 Commandments of Crowdfunding

This is pretty straightforward, and hits home that you should have your fulfillment systems in place before you launch. If you do hit a snag in getting rewards to people, reach out to them and keep them in the loop.

How close to people come to their expected budgets?

The majority of projects delivered on their expected budget, with only a small proportion having large overruns.

I was honestly happy to read this. I had this experience, and many others who are non-celebrities do too. It is also important to note that careful budget planning is crucial to hitting your target as well.

How do successful creators promote their campaign?

I thought it might be useful for creators to understand the prevalence and impact of various methods of promoting your campaign. It was fairly common to do so:

- 17% of successful campaigns used paid advertising
- 5% used consultants
- 32% used press releases
- 18% used events
- 70% promoted on social media

However, provided your campaign meets its goal, I found no statistical additional benefit to hiring consultants or paying for advertising in helping raise extra money. There was a slight benefit to putting out a press release (an average of $70 in extra pledges). That doesn't mean that these promotional strategies won't help you reach your goal in the first place, however.

THE 10 COMMANDMENTS OF CROWDFUNDING

Now you know why I kept reiterating why social media was so important. This is your easiest and least expensive medium to getting the word out about your campaign. I again think each campaign is a little different, so don't rule out using the other options if you have the resources to do so. If you feel the need to use a consultant or hold an event, do it. Each campaign will have its own needs and will appeal to a different subset of people; you can and should tailor your needs to fit it. Just don't get lackadaisical with your social media.

Crowdfunding Campaign Checklist

1. **Community engagement prior to launch. Did you...**
   - ☐ ... interact with personal friends through social media and email?
   - ☐ ... connect with like-minded groups and bloggers through social media?
   - ☐ ... get your team in place?

2. **Consistency. Are your....**
   - ☐ ... campaign images all the same?
   - ☐ ... color schemes matching on all of your online pages?
   - ☐ ... pre-written posts and campaign updates clear? Do they have consistent messaging? What about hashtags?
   - ☐ ... does your video contain the same images, colors, and messaging that are on your website and social media pages?

3. **Video. Is your video...**
   - ☐ ... script written?
   - ☐ ... about 2-3 minutes long?
   - ☐ ... using music and images pertinent to the campaign?
   - ☐ ... picture and audio clear and easily understood?

4. **Personal and self-care...**

   Are you communicating to friends and family members your needs? Remember, this is a marathon not a sprint and you'll need to step away from the computer at times and rest. Have your plan in place, and give yourself the breathing room to be fully present to show up for your campaign.

THE 10 COMMANDMENTS OF CROWDFUNDING

About Cece Otto

Cecelia Otto (AKA "Cece") is a classically trained singer, composer, and author, with an Interdepartmental Dual Masters Degree in Vocal Performance and Composition from the Lamont School of Music at the University of Denver; she is the only recipient of this degree in the university's history. In 2013, she completed her cross-country musical journey *An American Songline*®, performing 30 concerts of vintage music on venues along America's first transcontinental road, the Lincoln Highway. Today, she is an in-demand performer who continues to share America's history through song, and is also a crowdfunding consultant. She lives in Portland, Oregon, with her husband and talkative cat, and has written a book and recorded an album based on her travels. The book and CD are both titled, "An American Songline: A Musical Journey Along the Lincoln Highway," and are available on Amazon, iTunes, CD Baby, and more.

The 10 Commandments of Crowdfunding

Dear Reader...

If you want to talk with me more about crowdfunding, please reach out to me via email at americansongline@gmail.com. You can also find me online on Facebook, LinkedIn, Twitter, YouTube, Instagram, as well as on my website www.americansongline.net. You can subscribe to my newsletter, and learn more about my upcoming engagements and travels.

Please note that I'm an independent author, and this means I don't have a marketing department or the exposure of being on bookshelves. If you enjoyed reading *The Ten Commandments of Crowdfunding*, please help spread the word by writing an Amazon review or telling a few friends about this book.

Thanks, and I look forward to hearing from you!
Cecelia "Cece" Otto

"Cece offered us concrete, actionable advice on many levels that was easy to follow. Strategically she helped us create a vision, a broad-based panoramic picture of what we wanted to achieve. Then as we crafted said vision, she categorically offered tactics we could employ to better promote and execute our plan. She helped us set an attainable goal amount and helped us target our efforts effectively to our audience. We are happy to report that not only did we reach our initial goal in only 14 days, but we exceeded our goal by 26%.

Had we not employed Cece's recommendations we feel we might not have even gotten funded. One of the tactics alone she recommended accounted for over 30% of our donations.

Having someone who has actually done the process, and guide us with warmth and precision was invaluable to our campaign. Cece knows what she is doing, and if you follow her battle-tested advice, you will likely get your project funded in short order."

~ Jerry Chrisman, The Tesla City Stories - a live onstage radio theater production based in Portland, Oregon

www.ingramcontent.com/pod-product-compliance
Lightning Source LLC
Chambersburg PA
CBHW071819200526
45169CB00018B/459